quick
PASTA
recipes

The Confident Cooking Promise of Success

Welcome to the world of Confident Cooking,
where recipes are double-tested by our team
of home economists to achieve a high standard
of success—and delicious results every time.

bay books

TEST KITCHEN PERFECTION

You'll never make a wrong move with one of our step-by-step cookbooks. Our team of home economists has tested and refined the recipes so that you can create fabulous food in your own kitchen. Follow our easy instructions and step-by-step photographs and you'll feel like there is a master chef in the kitchen guiding you every step of the way.

All recipes are double-tested by our team of home economists. When we test our recipes, we rate them for ease of preparation. The following cookery ratings are on the recipes in this book, making them easy to use and understand.

A single Cooking with Confidence symbol indicates a recipe that is simple and generally quick to make—perfect for beginners.

Two symbols indicate the need for just a little more care and a little more time.

Three symbols indicate special dishes that need more investment in time, care and patience—but the results are worth it.

The Publisher thanks the following for their assistance: Corso De' Fiori, Country Road, Lincraft, Smeg Appliances, Witchery, Chief Australia, Breville Holdings Pty Ltd, Kambrook, Sheldon & Hammond, Bertolli Olive Oil, Southcorp Appliances.

Front cover: Spaghetti with smoked tuna and olives (page 61).
Inside front cover: Cavatelli with pecorino and a herb sauce (page 22).
Back cover: Orecchiette with spiced pumpkin and yoghurt (page 25).

CONTENTS

Top: *Veal tortellini with baked pumpkin and basil butter (page 77).* **Bottom:** *Warm pasta and smoked salmon stack (page 108), Rich cheese macaroni (page 33).*

PERFECT PASTA

THROW SOME PASTA INTO A POT OF BOILING WATER AND WHILE IT BUBBLES AWAY, COOK UP A SIMPLE SAUCE AND YOU HAVE A DELICIOUSLY EASY MEAL.

USING THIS BOOK

There are five main shapes of pasta: short, curly, long, filled and flat. For something a little different, we have divided our recipes into chapters that reflect the shape of the pasta they use. The same pasta may go by different names around the world, so, to help you identify the pasta shapes we have used, there is a helpful mini glossary at the start of each chapter. The glossary not only helps identify the different pasta types, but also gives some possible substitutions.

STORING PASTA

Dried pasta can be stored in a cool dry place for months. Fresh pasta must be refrigerated and won't keep for very long, so buy it as you need it. Filled pasta is best bought a day or so before you need it, but some vacuum-packed filled pastas can be kept for up to 3 weeks (check the use-by date). It can be frozen in a single layer between sheets of plastic wrap for up to 3 months but creamy fillings don't freeze well.

MATCHING SAUCE TO PASTA

With up to 300 different pasta shapes, it can be confusing knowing which sauce to serve with which pasta shape. A basic rule to remember is that a chunky pasta is best with a chunky sauce and a thin pasta is best with a thin sauce. Chunky pasta shapes enable you to pick up the sauce with the pasta. Smooth, slender pasta shapes will not hold a chunky sauce but will suit a sauce of olive oil or a fresh tomato sauce. Tiny pasta such as ditalini or stelline are usually used in soups.

HOW MUCH PASTA?

As pasta varies so much in shape, size and type, it is hard to be specific about how much pasta you need per serve. The chart below gives some basic guidelines about how much pasta to provide.

	STARTER	MAIN
Fresh pasta	85 g/3 oz	140 g/5 oz
Dried pasta	60 g/2½ oz	115 g/4 oz
Filled pasta	125 g/4½ oz	150 g/5½ oz

COOKING PASTA

Pasta should be cooked in a large, deep saucepan of water to allow room for expansion and to prevent it sticking together. Allow about 6 litres (24 cups) of water for every 500 g (1 lb 2 oz) pasta, but never use less than 4 litres (16 cups). Filled pasta and large pasta, such as lasagne, will need more water (9–12 litres/36–48 cups), as they are more likely to stick.

If you need to cook large amounts of pasta, cook up to 1 kg (2 lb 4 oz) of pasta per saucepan.

Always bring the water to the boil before stirring in the pasta. When the water comes back to the boil, begin timing, stirring often once the pasta softens a little. Test the pasta just prior to the final cooking time.

Adding oil to the pasta while cooking contributes very little, but seasoning the water with a little salt can add to the flavour. This is entirely a matter of personal preference.

COOKING TIME

Cooking times for pasta vary enormously depending on the size, shape and freshness of the pasta. Generally, the fresher the pasta, the shorter the cooking time. Fresh pasta from a delicatessen or pasta shop usually only needs 1–2 minutes. Vacuum-packed fresh pasta from the supermarket requires a little longer— about 6 minutes. Dried pasta varies depending on the size and shape but because it needs rehydrating as well as cooking, it usually takes longer than fresh pasta. For the most accurate times for all pasta, follow the instructions on the packet.

The best way to ensure pasta is cooked is to taste it. The pasta should be just tender, not at all raw or soft and gluggy. This is referred to in Italian as *al dente* which literally means 'to the tooth'.

SERVING UP

Once the pasta is cooked, it is important to drain it in a colander and then turn it either into a heated dish, the pan with the sauce or back into its cooking pan.

Don't overdrain the pasta: it needs to be a little wet for the sauce to coat it well. Never leave pasta sitting in the colander or it will clump together. A little olive oil or butter tossed through drained pasta will prevent it from sticking together.

Never rinse the pasta unless stated in the recipe: it is usually only rinsed if used in a baked meal or served cold in a salad because the starches released in cooking the pasta help it meld beautifully with the sauce.

Timing is essential when preparing a pasta meal. The sauce should be ready as soon as possible after the pasta is cooked because pasta continues to cook if left to sit around and can become soggy and unappetizing.

CAVATELLI

CONCHIGLIE

DITALINI

FARFALLE

MACARONI

ORECCHIETTE

ORZO

PASTA GNOCCHI

short

These pasta shapes refuse to be overlooked: their versatility means they can be used in almost any meal. Add your favourite sauce and they stand tall.

PENNE

RIGATONI

RISONI

ROTELLE

CAVATELLI: Made from 2–3 cm (3/4–1 1/4 inch) pieces of dough pressed and pushed with the thumb to make a curved and slightly hollowed oval shape. It is ideal with vegetable sauces, rich tomato sauces and seafood. Replace with orecchiette, pasta gnocchi or sardi (not shown).

CONCHIGLIE (shells): There are three sizes. *Conchiglie* is the most common of the shell pastas and is of a medium size with a ribbed surface that collects a lot of sauce. You can use pasta gnocchi or orecchiette instead. *Conchigliette* is the smallest; usually used in soups. Substitute ditalini or stelline (not shown). *Conchiglione* is the largest and is often stuffed (see page 73 for more information).

DITALINI: One of several tiny pasta shapes that are mainly used in soups, ditalini is a tiny tube-shaped pasta that can either have a smooth or ribbed surface. You can use any of the tiny pastas, such as the little star pasta, stelline (not shown), or orzo.

FARFALLE: The name means butterfly in Italian, which refers to its pretty shape. It is best with thick or chunky sauces, which catch in the folds. You can also use a similar-sized pasta, such as fusilli (page 31) or penne.

MACARONI: Very similar to elbow macaroni (page 31) but without the curve. Macaroni, otherwise known as straight macaroni, is a small tube pasta usually used in soups and bakes. The best substitute is elbow macaroni; you can also use cotelli or garganelli (page 31).

ORECCHIETTE: Orecchiette means little ears in Italian, and the name of the pasta is a typically literal description of the shape—although some brands look more like curls than ears. It is best with thick or chunky sauces. You can substitute cavatelli, conchiglie or pasta gnocchi.

ORZO: In Italian, orzo means barley and the pasta is so-called because of its similarity in appearance to grains of barley. It is mainly used in clear soups, but it can also be used as a substitute for rice in risotto. It is a little bigger than risoni.

PASTA GNOCCHI: Not to be confused with the potato dumplings of the same name, pasta gnocchi is, as the name suggests, a pasta of a similar shape to potato gnocchi. The curves of the pasta make is especially suitable to being served with thick or chunky sauces. Some suitable replacements are cavatelli, conchiglie or orecchiette.

PENNE: A popular quill-shaped tube, sometimes ribbed and sometimes plain. It is usually about 4 cm (1 1/2 inch) long. It is best with thick or chunky sauces. You can replace it with a pasta of a similar size, such as fusilli, garganelli (page 31), passatelli (not shown), or rigatoni.

RIGATONI: There are many sizes of this tube-shaped pasta. The largest size is usually stuffed and baked, but the other sizes are all interchangeable. The ribbed walls of the pasta catch the sauce. You can substitute large fusilli (page 31), penne or rotelle.

RISONI: This is a small pasta that looks very similar to arborio rice. It is best used in soups, bakes and casseroles or when used in a risotto instead of rice. Stelline (not shown), orzo or ditalini will work well in the same recipes (but not in risotto).

ROTELLE: Otherwise known as ruote, this pasta has a very distinctive wheel shape. Traditionally it is served with a tomato sauce, but it is suitable for most sauces. If you need to replace it, use a pasta of similar size, such as cresti di gallo (page 31), farfalle or rigatoni.

WARM CHICKEN AND PASTA SALAD

Preparation time: 15 minutes
Cooking time: 15 minutes
Serves 4

375 g (13 oz) penne
100 ml (3¹/2 fl oz) olive oil
4 slender eggplants (aubergines),
    thinly sliced on the diagonal
2 chicken breast fillets
2 teaspoons lemon juice
15 g (¹/2 cup) chopped fresh
    flat-leaf (Italian) parsley
270 g (9³/4 oz) chargrilled red
    capsicum (pepper), drained and
    sliced (see Note)

155 g (5¹/2 oz) fresh asparagus,
    trimmed, blanched and cut into
    5 cm (2 inch) lengths
85 g (3 oz) semi-dried (sun-blushed)
    tomatoes, finely sliced

1 Cook the pasta in a large saucepan of boiling water until *al dente*. Drain, return to the pan and keep warm. Heat 2 tablespoons of the oil in a large frying pan over high heat and cook the eggplant for 4–5 minutes, or until golden and cooked through.

2 Heat a lightly oiled chargrill pan (griddle) over high heat and cook the chicken for 5 minutes each side, or until browned and cooked through. Cut into thick slices. Put the lemon juice, parsley and remaining oil in a small jar and shake well. Return the pasta to the heat, toss through the dressing, chicken, eggplant, capsicum, asparagus and tomato until well mixed and warmed through. Season with black pepper. Serve warm with grated Parmesan, if desired.

NUTRITION PER SERVE
Fat 28 g; Protein 50 g; Carbohydrate 71.5 g; Dietary Fibre 7.5 g; Cholesterol 113.5 mg; 3120 kJ (745 Cal)

COOK'S FILE
Note: Jars of chargrilled capsicum can be bought at the supermarket; otherwise, visit your local deli.

RISONI RISOTTO WITH MUSHROOMS AND PANCETTA

Preparation time: 15 minutes
Cooking time: 35 minutes
Serves 4–6

25 g (1 oz) butter
2 garlic cloves, finely chopped
150 g (5 1/2 oz) piece pancetta, diced
400 g (14 oz) button mushrooms, sliced
500 g (1 lb 2 oz) risoni
1 litre (4 cups) chicken stock
125 ml (1/2 cup) cream
50 g (1/2 cup) finely grated Parmesan cheese
4 tablespoons finely chopped fresh flat-leaf (Italian) parsley

1 Melt the butter in a saucepan, add the garlic and cook over medium heat for 30 seconds, then increase the heat to high, add the pancetta and cook for 3–5 minutes, or until crisp. Add the mushrooms and cook for 3–5 minutes, or until softened.

2 Add the risoni, stir until coated in the mixture. Add the stock and bring to the boil. Reduce the heat to medium and cook, covered, for 15–20 minutes, or until nearly all the liquid has evaporated and the risoni is tender.

3 Stir in the cream and cook, uncovered, for a further 3 minutes, stirring occasionally until the cream is absorbed. Stir in 35 g (1/3 cup) of the Parmesan and all the parsley and season to taste. Divide among four serving bowls and serve sprinkled with the remaining Parmesan.

NUTRITION PER SERVE (6)
Fat 20 g; Protein 21.5 g; Carbohydrate 59.5 g; Dietary Fibre 4.5 g; Cholesterol 60 mg; 2110 kJ (505 Cal)

1

2

3

GREEK PASTA SALAD

Preparation time: 10 minutes
Cooking time: 45 minutes
Serves 4

4 Roma (plum) tomatoes, quartered
1 tablespoon chopped fresh oregano
500 g (1 lb 2 oz) rigatoni
250 g (9 oz) marinated soft feta cheese
1 red onion, halved and sliced
1 tablespoon capers in salt, rinsed
    and patted dry (see Note)
2½ tablespoons red wine vinegar
15 g (½ cup) chopped fresh flat-leaf
    (Italian) parsley
2 tablespoons ready-made olive
    tapenade

1 Preheat the oven to 180°C (350°F/ Gas 4). Place the tomatoes, cut-side-up, on a baking tray, sprinkle with 1 teaspoon of the oregano and season with salt and pepper. Roast for 30–40 minutes, or until soft and caramelized.

2 Meanwhile, cook the pasta in a large saucepan of boiling water until *al dente*. Drain the pasta and return to the pan to keep warm.

3 Drain and crumble the feta, reserving the oil and herbs. Heat 2 teaspoons of the reserved oil in a small frying pan, add the onion and cook over medium heat for 2–3 minutes, or until soft, then add the capers and cook for a further minute. Combine the rest of the reserved oil with the vinegar and stir into the pan. Remove from the heat and stir through the pasta, adding the remaining oregano and the parsley. Divide among four serving plates and top with the tomato, feta and the tapenade.

NUTRITION PER SERVE
Fat 16 g; Protein 26.5 g; Carbohydrate 89 g; Dietary Fibre 6 g; Cholesterol 43 mg; 2570 kJ (615 Cal)

COOK'S FILE
Note: You can buy capers in salt from delicatessens—they are smaller than normal capers and are kept in salt rather than brine. If you want to use capers in brine, buy baby capers and drain them before use.

PASTA GNOCCHI WITH SAUSAGE AND TOMATO

Preparation time: 15 minutes
Cooking time: 20 minutes
Serves 4–6

500 g (1 lb 2 oz) pasta gnocchi
2 tablespoons olive oil
400 g (14 oz) thin Italian sausages
1 red onion, finely chopped
2 garlic cloves, finely chopped
2 x 400 g (14 oz) cans chopped
   tomatoes
1 teaspoon caster (superfine)
   sugar

35 g (1¼ oz) fresh basil, torn
45 g (½ cup) grated pecorino cheese

1 Cook the pasta in a large saucepan of boiling water until *al dente*. Drain and return the pasta to the pan. Meanwhile, heat 2 teaspoons of the oil in a large frying pan. Add the sausages and cook, turning, for 5 minutes, or until well browned and cooked through. Drain on paper towels, then slice when they have cooled enough to touch. Keep warm.
2 Wipe clean the frying pan and heat the remaining oil. Add the onion and garlic and cook over medium heat for 2 minutes, or until the onion has softened. Add the tomato, sugar and 250 ml (1 cup) water and season well with ground black pepper. Reduce the heat and simmer for 12 minutes, or until thickened and reduced a little.
3 Pour the sauce over the cooked pasta and stir through the sausage, then the basil and half of the cheese. Divide among serving plates and serve hot with the remaining cheese sprinkled over the top.

NUTRITION PER SERVE (6)
Fat 29.5 g; Protein 17 g; Carbohydrate 29.5 g; Dietary Fibre 4 g; Cholesterol 57.5 mg; 1905 kJ (455 Cal)

1

2

3

ROASTED ORANGE SWEET POTATO AND DITALINI PATTIES

Preparation time: 15 minutes
Cooking time: 1 hour 10 minutes
Serves 4

2 orange sweet potatoes
   (about 800 g/1 lb 12 oz in total)
90 g (1/2 cup) ditalini
30 g (1 oz) toasted pine nuts
2 garlic cloves, crushed
4 tablespoons finely chopped basil
50 g (1/2 cup) grated Parmesan
   cheese
35 g (1/3 cup) dry breadcrumbs
plain (all-purpose) flour, for dusting
olive oil, for shallow-frying

1 Preheat the oven to 250°C (500°F/ Gas 10). Pierce the whole orange sweet potatoes several times with a fork, then place in a roasting tin and roast for about 1 hour, or until soft. Remove from the oven and cool. Meanwhile, cook the pasta in a large saucepan of boiling water until *al dente*. Drain and rinse under running water.
2 Peel the sweet potato and mash the flesh with a potato masher or fork, then add the pine nuts, garlic, basil, Parmesan, breadcrumbs and the pasta and combine. Season.
3 Shape the mixture into eight even patties (about 1.5 cm/5/8 inch thick) with floured hands, then lightly dust the patties with flour. Heat the oil in a large frying pan and cook the

patties in batches over medium heat for 2 minutes each side, or until golden and heated through. Drain on crumpled paper towels, sprinkle with salt and serve immediately. Great with a fresh green salad.

NUTRITION PER SERVE
Fat 15 g; Protein 13.5 g; Carbohydrate 51 g; Dietary Fibre 5.5 g; Cholesterol 12 mg; 1650 kJ (395 Cal)

COOK'S FILE
Note: To save time, drop spoonfuls of the mixture into the pan and flatten with an oiled spatula.
Serving suggestion: The patties are great with aïoli—mix 1 clove of crushed garlic into 90 g (1/3 cup) good-quality whole-egg mayonnaise with a squeeze of lemon juice and season.

TOMATO DITALINI SOUP

Preparation time: 15 minutes
Cooking time: 20 minutes
Serves 4

2 tablespoons olive oil
1 large onion, finely chopped
2 celery sticks, finely chopped
3 vine-ripened tomatoes
1.5 litres (6 cups) chicken or
    vegetable stock
90 g (½ cup) ditalini
2 tablespoons chopped fresh
    flat-leaf (Italian) parsley

1 Heat the oil in a large saucepan over medium heat. Add the onion and celery and cook for 5 minutes, or until they have softened.
2 Score a cross in the base of each tomato, then place in a bowl of boiling water for 1 minute. Plunge into cold water and peel the skin away from the cross. Halve the tomatoes and scoop out the seeds. Roughly chop the flesh. Add the stock and tomato to the onion mixture and bring to the boil. Add the pasta and cook for 10 minutes, or until *al dente*. Season and sprinkle with parsley.

NUTRITION PER SERVE
Fat 11 g; Protein 8 g; Carbohydrate 23 g;
Dietary Fibre 3.5 g; Cholesterol 0 mg;
925 kJ (220 Cal)

PASTA DI STALLA
(Pasta from the barn)

Preparation time: 10 minutes
Cooking time: 15 minutes
Serves 4

375 g (13 oz) orecchiette
1 large potato, cut into 1.5 cm
    (5/8 inch) cubes
400 g (14 oz) broccoli
80 ml (1/3 cup) olive oil
3 garlic cloves, crushed
1 small red chilli, finely chopped
2 x 400 g (14 oz) cans chopped
    tomatoes
25 g (1/4 cup) grated pecorino cheese

1 Bring a large saucepan of salted water to the boil and cook the pasta and potato for 8–10 minutes, or until the pasta is *al dente*. Drain and return to the pan. Meanwhile, trim the broccoli into florets and discard the stems. Place in a saucepan of boiling water and cook for 1–2 minutes, then drain and plunge into iced water. Drain and add to the pasta and potato.
2 Heat the oil in a saucepan, add the garlic and chilli and cook for 30 seconds. Add the tomato and simmer for 5 minutes, or until slightly reduced and thickened. Season to taste with salt and pepper.
3 Pour the tomato mixture over the pasta, potato and broccoli. Toss well and stir over low heat until warmed through. Serve sprinkled with grated pecorino cheese.

NUTRITION PER SERVE
Fat 21.5 g; Protein 19.5 g; Carbohydrate 76.5 g; Dietary Fibre 10.5 g; Cholesterol 5.5 mg; 2445 kJ (585 Cal)

PENNE WITH PUMPKIN, BAKED RICOTTA AND PROSCIUTTO

Preparation time: 15 minutes
Cooking time: 15 minutes
Serves 4

500 g (1 lb 2 oz) penne
460 g (1 lb) butternut pumpkin (squash),
    cut in 1 cm (¹/2 inch) cubes
60 ml (¹/4 cup) extra virgin olive oil

2 garlic cloves, crushed
100 g (3¹/2 oz) semi-dried (sun-
    blushed) tomatoes, chopped
4 slices prosciutto, chopped
250 g (9 oz) baked ricotta cheese,
    cut into 1 cm (¹/2 inch) cubes
3 tablespoons shredded fresh basil

1 Cook the pasta in a large saucepan of boiling water until *al dente*. Drain. Meanwhile, cook the pumpkin in a saucepan of boiling water for 10–12 minutes, or until just tender, then drain well.

2 Heat the oil in a large saucepan, add the garlic and cook over medium heat for 30 seconds. Add the tomato, prosciutto, pumpkin and penne and toss gently over low heat for 1–2 minutes, or until heated through.

3 Add the baked ricotta and the basil, season and serve immediately.

NUTRITION PER SERVE
Fat 23 g; Protein 28.5 g; Carbohydrate 99 g;
Dietary Fibre 8.5 g; Cholesterol 37 mg;
3020 kJ (720 Cal)

CONCHIGLIETTE WITH WALNUT PESTO

Preparation time: 15 minutes
Cooking time: 15 minutes
Serves 4–6

125 g (4¹/₂ oz) day-old crusty bread,
    crusts removed
185 g (1¹/₂ cups) walnut pieces
500 g (1 lb 2 oz) conchigliette
30 g (¹/₂ cup) fresh basil, roughly
    chopped
2–3 garlic cloves, peeled
1 small red chilli, seeded and
    roughly chopped
¹/₂ teaspoon finely grated lemon zest
60 ml (¹/₄ cup) lemon juice
125 ml (¹/₂ cup) olive oil

1   Preheat the oven to 160°C (315°F/ Gas 2–3). Cut the bread into 2 cm (³/4 inch) thick slices and place on a baking tray with the walnuts. Bake for 8–10 minutes, or until the bread is dried out a little and the walnuts are lightly toasted. Don't overcook the walnuts or they will be bitter.
2   Meanwhile, cook the pasta in a large saucepan of boiling water until *al dente*. Drain and return the pasta to the pan.
3   Break the bread into chunks and place in a food processor. Add the walnuts, basil, garlic, chilli, lemon zest and juice. Use the pulse button to chop the mixture without forming a paste. Transfer to a bowl and stir in the oil. Toss the walnut mixture through the pasta, then season.

NUTRITION PER SERVE (6)
Fat 38.5 g; Protein 15 g; Carbohydrate 69.5 g; Dietary Fibre 7 g; Cholesterol 0 mg; 2870 kJ (685 Cal)

COOK'S FILE
Note: Don't add the oil to the food processor or the pesto will lose its crunchy texture.

1

2

3

FARFALLE WITH SPINACH AND BACON

Preparation time: 10 minutes
Cooking time: 15 minutes
Serves 4

400 g (14 oz) farfalle
2 tablespoons extra virgin olive oil
250 g (9 oz) bacon, chopped
1 red onion, finely chopped
250 g (9 oz) baby English spinach leaves, stalks trimmed
1–2 tablespoons sweet chilli sauce (optional)
35 g (¼ cup) crumbled goat's feta cheese

1 Cook the pasta in a large saucepan of boiling water until *al dente*, then drain and return to the saucepan.

Meanwhile, heat the oil in a frying pan, add the bacon and cook over medium heat for 3 minutes, or until golden. Add the onion and cook for a further 4 minutes, or until softened. Toss the spinach leaves through the onion and bacon mixture for 30 seconds, or until just wilted.

2 Add the bacon and spinach mixture to the drained pasta, then stir in the sweet chilli sauce. Season to taste with salt and ground black pepper and toss well. Spoon into warm bowls and scatter with the crumbled feta. Serve immediately.

NUTRITION PER SERVE
Fat 19 g; Protein 28 g; Carbohydrate 73 g; Dietary Fibre 7 g; Cholesterol 42 mg; 2415 kJ (575 Cal)

1

2

RICOTTA, EGGPLANT AND PASTA TIMBALES

Preparation time: 15 minutes
Cooking time: 45 minutes
Makes 4

125 ml (½ cup) light olive oil
1 large eggplant (aubergine),
    sliced lengthways into 1 cm
    (½ inch) slices
200 g (7 oz) straight macaroni
1 small onion, finely chopped
2 garlic cloves, crushed
400 g (14 oz) can chopped
    tomatoes
400 g (14 oz) ricotta cheese
80 g (1 cup) coarsely grated
    Parmesan cheese

15 g (½ cup) shredded fresh basil,
    plus extra to garnish

1 Preheat the oven to 180°C (350°F/ Gas 4). Heat 2 tablespoons of the oil in a non-stick frying pan and cook the eggplant in three batches over medium heat for 2–3 minutes each side, or until golden, adding 2 tablespoons of the oil with each batch. Remove from the pan and drain on crumpled paper towels. Meanwhile, cook the pasta in a large saucepan of boiling water until *al dente*. Drain and set aside.

2 Add the onion and garlic to the frying pan and cook over medium heat for 2–3 minutes, or until just golden. Add the tomato and cook for 5 minutes, or until the sauce is pulpy and most of the liquid has evaporated. Season, then remove from the heat.

3 Combine the ricotta, Parmesan and basil, then mix in the pasta. Line the base and sides of four 375 ml (1½ cup) ramekins with eggplant, trimming any overhanging pieces. Top with half the pasta mix, pressing down firmly. Spoon on the tomato sauce, then cover with the remaining pasta. Bake for 10–15 minutes, or until heated and golden on top. Stand for 5 minutes, then run a knife around the side to loosen the timbale. Invert onto plates, garnish with basil and serve with a side salad and bread.

NUTRITION PER TIMBALE
Fat 40 g; Protein 25.5 g; Carbohydrate 42.5 g; Dietary Fibre 6 g; Cholesterol 67 mg; 2645 kJ (630 Cal)

1

2

3

CREAMY PASTA GNOCCHI WITH PEAS AND PROSCIUTTO

Preparation time: 15 minutes
Cooking time: 20 minutes
Serves 4

100 g (3¹/₂ oz) thinly sliced prosciutto
3 teaspoons oil
2 eggs
250 ml (1 cup) cream
35 g (¹/₃ cup) grated Parmesan cheese
2 tablespoons chopped fresh
    flat-leaf (Italian) parsley
1 tablespoon chopped fresh chives
250 g (9 oz) fresh or frozen peas
500 g (1 lb 2 oz) pasta gnocchi

1 Cut the prosciutto into 5 mm (¹/₄ inch) wide strips. Heat the oil in a frying pan over medium heat, cook the prosciutto for 2 minutes, or until crisp. Drain on paper towels. Place the eggs, cream, Parmesan and herbs in a bowl and whisk well.

2 Bring a large saucepan of salted water to the boil. Add the peas and cook for 5 minutes, or until just tender. Leaving the pan on the heat, use a slotted spoon and transfer the peas to the bowl of cream mixture, and then add 60 ml (¹/₄ cup) of the cooking liquid to the same bowl. Using a potato masher or the back of a fork, roughly mash the peas.

3 Add the gnocchi to the boiling water and cook until *al dente*. Drain well, then return to the pan. Add the cream mixture, then warm through over low heat, gently stirring for about 30 seconds until the gnocchi is coated in the sauce. Season. Divide among warmed plates, top with the prosciutto and serve immediately.

NUTRITION PER SERVE
Fat 32.5 g; Protein 21 g; Carbohydrate 41 g; Dietary Fibre 6 g; Cholesterol 201 mg; 2260 kJ (540 Cal)

COOK'S FILE
Note: Be careful not to overheat or cook for too long as the egg will begin to set and the result will look like a scrambled egg sauce.

1

2

3

PASTA E FAGIOLI
(Hearty pasta and bean soup)

Preparation time: 15 minutes
Cooking time: 20 minutes
Serves 4

1 tablespoon olive oil
1 onion, finely chopped
3 garlic cloves, crushed
2 x 290 g (10 oz) cans mixed beans, drained
1.75 litres (7 cups) chicken stock (see Note)
100 g (3½ oz) conchigliette
1 tablespoon chopped fresh tarragon

1 Heat the oil in a saucepan over low heat. Add the onion and cook for 5 minutes, then add the garlic and cook for a further 1 minute, stirring frequently. Add the beans and chicken stock, cover the pan with a lid, increase the heat and bring to the boil. Add the pasta and cook until *al dente*. Stir in the tarragon, then season with salt and ground black pepper. Serve with crusty bread.

NUTRITION PER SERVE
Fat 6.5 g; Protein 12 g; Carbohydrate 34 g; Dietary Fibre 8 g; Cholesterol 0 mg; 1015 kJ (240 Cal)

COOK'S FILE
Note: The flavour of this soup is really enhanced by using a good-quality stock. Either make your own or use the tetra packs of liquid stock that are available at the supermarket.

1

ZUCCHINI PASTA BAKE

Preparation time: 15 minutes
Cooking time: 40 minutes
Serves 4

200 g (7 oz) risoni
40 g (1½ oz) butter
4 spring onions (scallions), thinly sliced
400 g (14 oz) zucchini (courgettes), grated
4 eggs
125 ml (½ cup) cream
100 g (3½ oz) ricotta cheese (see Note)
100 g (⅔ cup) grated mozzarella cheese
75 g (¾ cup) grated Parmesan cheese

1 Preheat the oven to 180°C (350°F/ Gas 4). Cook the pasta in a large saucepan of boiling water until *al dente*. Drain well. Meanwhile, heat the butter in a frying pan, cook the spring onion for 1 minute, then add the zucchini and cook for a further 4 minutes, or until soft. Cool slightly.
2 Combine the eggs, cream, ricotta, mozzarella, risoni and half of the Parmesan well. Stir in the zucchini mixture. Season. Spoon into four 500 ml (2 cup) greased ovenproof dishes, but not to the brim. Sprinkle with the remaining Parmesan and cook for 25–30 minutes, or until firm and golden.

NUTRITION PER SERVE
Fat 40.5 g; Protein 28.5 g; Carbohydrate 39 g; Dietary Fibre 4.5 g; Cholesterol 310.5 mg; 2635 kJ (630 Cal)

COOK'S FILE
Note: With such simple flavours, it is important to use good-quality fresh ricotta from the delicatessen or the deli section of your local supermarket.

CAVATELLI WITH PECORINO AND A HERB SAUCE

Preparation time: 10 minutes
Cooking time: 15 minutes
Serves 4

400 g (14 oz) cavatelli
80 g (2³/₄ oz) butter
2 garlic cloves, crushed
3 tablespoons chopped fresh chives
3 tablespoons shredded fresh basil
1 tablespoon shredded fresh sage
1 teaspoon fresh thyme
60 ml (¹/₄ cup) warm vegetable stock
60 g (²/₃ cup) firmly packed grated
    pecorino cheese

1 Cook the pasta in a large saucepan of boiling water until *al dente*. Meanwhile, heat the butter in a small saucepan over medium heat, add the garlic and cook for 1 minute, or until fragrant. Add the chives, basil, sage and thyme and cook for a further minute.

2 Drain the pasta and return to the pan. Add the herb mixture and stock. Return to the heat for 2–3 minutes, or until warmed through. Season to taste with salt and ground black pepper. Add the grated pecorino and stir until well combined. Divide among four warm serving bowls and garnish with sage leaves, if desired.

NUTRITION PER SERVE
Fat 21.5 g; Protein 16 g; Carbohydrate 71 g; Dietary Fibre 5.5 g; Cholesterol 64.5 mg; 2280 kJ (545 Cal)

COOK'S FILE
Note: Pecorino is sheep's milk cheese with a sharp flavour. If unavailable, use Parmesan instead.

1

2

PENNE WITH VEAL RAGOUT

Preparation time: 15 minutes
Cooking time: 2 hours 40 minutes
Serves 4

2 onions, sliced
2 bay leaves, crushed
1.5 kg (3 lb 5 oz) veal shin, cut into
    osso bucco pieces (see Note)
250 ml (1 cup) red wine
2 x 400 g (14 oz) cans crushed
    tomatoes
375 ml (1¹/₂ cups) beef stock
2 teaspoons chopped fresh rosemary
400 g (14 oz) penne
140 g (1 cup) frozen peas

1 Preheat the oven to 220°C (425°F/Gas 7). Scatter the onion over the bottom of a large roasting tin (we used 32 x 23 cm/13 x 9 inch), lightly spray with oil and place the bay leaves and veal pieces on top. Season. Roast for 10–15 minutes, or until the veal is browned. Ensure the onion doesn't burn.

2 Pour the wine over the veal and return to the oven for a further 5 minutes. Reduce the heat to 180°C (350°F/Gas 4), remove the tin from the oven and pour on the tomato, stock and 1 teaspoon of the rosemary. Cover with foil and return to the oven. Cook for 2 hours, or until the veal is starting to fall from the bone. Remove the foil and cook for a further 15 minutes, or until the meat loosens away from the bone and the liquid has evaporated slightly.

3 Cook the pasta in a large saucepan of boiling water until *al dente*. Meanwhile, remove the veal from the oven and cool slightly. Add the peas and remaining rosemary and place over a hotplate. Cook over medium heat for 5 minutes, or until the peas are cooked. Drain the pasta, divide among four bowls and top with the ragout.

NUTRITION PER SERVE
Fat 5 g; Protein 51.5 g; Carbohydrate 81 g;
Dietary Fibre 10 g; Cholesterol 125 mg;
2605 kJ (620 Cal)

COOK'S FILE
Notes: Most butchers sell veal shin cut into osso bucco pieces. If sold whole, ask the butcher to cut into pieces for you (about 3–4 cm/1¹/₄–1¹/₂ inch thick). It is also available at some supermarkets. Either remove the meat from the bone before serving, or leave it on.

1

2

3

CAJUN SCALLOPS, CONCHIGLIETTE AND BUTTERY CORN SAUCE

Preparation time: 15 minutes
Cooking time: 15 minutes
Serves 4

350 g (12 oz) conchigliette or conchiglie
20 large scallops, without roe
2 tablespoons Cajun spice mix
2 tablespoons corn oil
250 g (9 oz) butter
3 garlic cloves, crushed
400 g (14 oz) can corn kernels, drained
60 ml (¼ cup) lime juice

4 tablespoons finely chopped fresh coriander (cilantro) leaves

1 Cook the pasta in a large saucepan of boiling water until *al dente*. Drain and return to the pan to keep warm. Meanwhile, pat the scallops dry with paper towel and lightly coat in the spice mix. Heat the oil in a frying pan and cook the scallops for 1 minute each side over high heat (ensuring they are well spaced), then remove from the pan, cover and keep warm.
2 Reduce the heat to medium, add the butter and cook for 4 minutes, or until foaming and golden brown. Remove from the heat, add the garlic, corn and lime juice. Gently toss the corn mixture through the pasta with

2 tablespoons of the coriander and season well. Divide among four serving plates, top with the scallops, drizzle with any juices and sprinkle with the remaining coriander.

NUTRITION PER SERVE
Fat 60.5 g; Protein 20 g; Carbohydrate 75 g; Dietary Fibre 7 g; Cholesterol 174.5 mg; 3850 kJ (920 Cal)

COOK'S FILE
Notes: Do not crowd scallops during cooking—they will release all their juices, causing them to stew and toughen. Use a good-quality Cajun spice mix. To achieve the most delicious flavours, don't use a non-stick frying pan—they can prevent the butter from browning and the juices from caramelizing.

1

2

ORECCHIETTE WITH SPICED PUMPKIN AND YOGHURT

Preparation time: 15 minutes
Cooking time: 35 minutes
Serves 6

1 kg (2 lb 4 oz) pumpkin, cut into
   2 cm (³/4 inch) cubes
80 ml (¹/3 cup) olive oil
500 g (1 lb 2 oz) orecchiette
2 garlic cloves, crushed
1 teaspoon dried chilli flakes
1 teaspoon coriander (cilantro) seeds,
   crushed
1 tablespoon cumin seeds, crushed
200 g (7 oz) Greek-style natural
   yoghurt
3 tablespoons chopped fresh
   coriander (cilantro) leaves

1 Preheat the oven to 200°C (400°F/Gas 6). Toss the pumpkin in 2 tablespoons of the oil, place in a roasting tin and cook for 30 minutes, or until golden and crisp, tossing halfway through.

2 Meanwhile, cook the pasta in a large saucepan of boiling water until *al dente*. Drain, then return to the pan.

3 Heat the remaining oil in a saucepan. Add the garlic, chilli, coriander and cumin and cook for 30 seconds, or until fragrant. Toss the spice mix and pumpkin through the pasta, then stir in the yoghurt and fresh coriander and season to taste with salt and ground black pepper. Divide among serving bowls and serve.

NUTRITION PER SERVE
Fat 15 g; Protein 14.5 g; Carbohydrate 71.5 g; Dietary Fibre 6.5 g; Cholesterol 5.5 mg; 2035 kJ (485 Cal)

ROTELLE WITH CHICKPEAS, TOMATO AND PARSLEY

Preparation time: 10 minutes
Cooking time: 15 minutes
Serves 4

375 g (13 oz) rotelle
1 tablespoon ground cumin
125 ml (1/2 cup) olive oil
1 red onion, halved and thinly sliced
3 garlic cloves, crushed
400 g (14 oz) can chickpeas, drained
3 large tomatoes, diced
15 g (1/2 cup) chopped fresh
  flat-leaf (Italian) parsley
60 ml (1/4 cup) lemon juice

1 Cook the pasta in a large saucepan of boiling water until *al dente*. Drain and return to the pan.

2 Meanwhile, heat a large frying pan over medium heat, add the cumin and cook, tossing, for 1 minute, or until fragrant. Remove from the pan. Heat half the oil in the same pan and cook the onion over medium heat for 2–3 minutes, or until soft. Stir in the garlic, chickpeas, tomato and parsley and stir until warmed through. Gently toss through the pasta.

3 Place the lemon juice, cumin and remaining oil in a jar with a lid and shake together well. Add the dressing to the saucepan with the pasta and chickpea mixture, return to the stove-top over low heat and stir until warmed through. Season well with salt and ground black pepper. Serve hot with grated Parmesan, or you can serve it cold. If serving cold, rinse the pasta under cold water before adding the chickpea mixture and do not return to the heat.

NUTRITION PER SERVE
Fat 27 g; Protein 17 g; Carbohydrate 80 g; Dietary Fibre 10 g; Cholesterol 0 mg; 2655 kJ (635 Cal)

1

2

3

PENNE WITH RUSTIC LENTIL SAUCE

Preparation time: 10 minutes
Cooking time: 30 minutes
Serves 4

1 litre (4 cups) chicken stock
350 g (12 oz) penne
80 ml (1/3 cup) virgin olive oil,
  plus extra for drizzling
1 onion, chopped
2 carrots, diced
3 celery sticks, diced
3 garlic cloves, crushed
1 tablespoon plus 1 teaspoon
  chopped fresh thyme
400 g (14 oz) can lentils, drained

1 Boil the chicken stock in a large saucepan for 10 minutes, or until reduced to 500 ml (2 cups) of liquid. Meanwhile, cook the pasta in a large saucepan of boiling water until *al dente*. Drain and toss with 2 tablespoons of the olive oil.

2 Heat the remaining oil in a large, deep frying pan, add the onion, carrot and celery and cook over medium heat for 10 minutes, or until browned. Add two thirds of the crushed garlic and 1 tablespoon of the thyme and cook for a further 1 minute. Add the stock, bring to the boil and cook for 8 minutes, or until reduced slightly and the vegetables are tender. Gently stir in the lentils until heated through.

3 Stir in the remaining garlic and thyme, and season with plenty of salt and ground black pepper—the stock should be slightly syrupy at this point. Combine the pasta with the lentil sauce in a large bowl, drizzle generously with virgin olive oil and serve with grated Parmesan, if desired.

NUTRITION PER SERVE
Fat 18 g; Protein 16.5 g; Carbohydrate 72 g; Dietary Fibre 9 g; Cholesterol 0 mg; 2165 kJ (515 Cal)

ORZO AND GREEK CHEESE BAKE

Preparation time: 15 minutes
Cooking time: 40 minutes
Serves 6

415 g (2 cups) orzo
60 g (2¼ oz) butter
6 spring onions (scallions), chopped
450 g (1 lb) English spinach, stems removed, rinsed well and chopped
2 tablespoons plain (all-purpose) flour
1.25 litres (5 cups) milk
250 g (9 oz) kefalotyri cheese, grated (see Note)
250 g (9 oz) marinated feta cheese, drained
3 tablespoons chopped fresh dill

1   Preheat the oven to 190°C (375°F/ Gas 5). Cook the pasta in a large pan of boiling water until *al dente*. Drain well, then return to the pan. Heat 20 g (½ oz) butter in a large pan over high heat and cook the spring onion for 30 seconds. Add the spinach and stir for 1 minute, or until wilted. Season; stir into the orzo.

2   Put the remaining butter in the saucepan in which the spinach was cooked. Melt over low heat, then stir in the flour and cook for 1 minute, or until pale and foaming. Remove from the heat and gradually stir in the milk. Return to the heat and stir constantly for 5 minutes, or until the sauce boils and thickens. Add two thirds of the kefalotyri and all of the feta and stir for 2 minutes until melted and well mixed. Remove from the heat and stir in the dill.

3   Combine the pasta mix with the cheese sauce, season and pour into a greased 2.5 litre (10 cup) ovenproof ceramic dish. Sprinkle the remaining cheese on top. Bake for 15 minutes.

NUTRITION PER SERVE
Fat 34 g; Protein 30.5 g; Carbohydrate 63 g; Dietary Fibre 6 g; Cholesterol 102.5 mg; 2835 kJ (680 Cal)

COOK'S FILE
Note: Kefalotyri is a hard sheep's cheese.

ORECCHIETTE WITH BROCCOLI, ANCHOVIES AND BASIL

Preparation time: 15 minutes
Cooking time: 25 minutes
Serves 4–6

600 g (1 lb 5 oz) broccoli, cut into florets
500 g (1 lb 2 oz) orecchiette
1 tablespoon olive oil
4 garlic cloves, finely chopped
8 anchovy fillets, roughly chopped
250 ml (1 cup) cream
30 g (1 cup) fresh basil, torn
2 teaspoons finely grated lemon zest
100 g (1 cup) grated Parmesan cheese

1 Blanch the broccoli in a large saucepan of boiling salted water for 3–4 minutes. Remove and plunge into chilled water. Drain well with a slotted spoon. Bring the water back to the boil and cook the pasta until *al dente*. Drain, reserving 2 tablespoons of the cooking water.

2 Meanwhile, heat the oil in a frying pan. Add the garlic and anchovies and cook over medium heat for 1–2 minutes, or until the garlic begins to turn golden. Add the broccoli and cook for a further 5 minutes. Add the cream and half the basil and cook for 10 minutes, or until the cream has reduced and slightly thickened and the broccoli is very tender.

3 Purée half the mixture in a food processor until nearly smooth, then return to the pan with the lemon zest, half the Parmesan and 2 tablespoons of the reserved water. Stir together well, then season with salt and ground black pepper. Add the warm pasta and remaining basil, and toss until well combined. Sprinkle with the remaining Parmesan and serve immediately.

NUTRITION PER SERVE (6)
Fat 28 g; Protein 22.5 g; Carbohydrate 60.5 g; Dietary Fibre 9 g; Cholesterol 76.5 mg; 2455 kJ (585 Cal)

1

2

3

COTELLI

CRESTI DI GALLO

ELBOW MACARONI

FRICELLI

FUSILLI

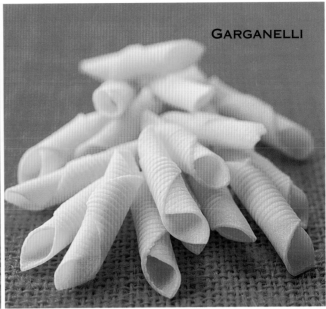

GARGANELLI

curly

The curls and swirls of curly pasta
shapes add interest to even the simplest of sauces.
The challenge is catching them with your fork!

COTELLI: Otherwise known as cavatappi, these hollow tubes of pasta are formed into curls or ringlets. Cotelli is best with thick or chunky sauces as the chunks of the sauce get caught up in the curls. You can substitute a similar-sized and shaped pasta, such as cresti di gallo, elbow macaroni or fusilli.

CRESTI DI GALLO: Named after the Italian word for 'cockscombs', the name of this pasta is a reference to the similarity in shape to the crest of a rooster. Its basic structure is similar to elbow macaroni with the addition of a ruffled frill on the outside edge of the pasta. It can be replaced by rotelle (page 7) or cotelli.

ELBOW MACARONI: The name elbow macaroni is an American term for short curved hollow tubes of pasta. It is part of the macaroni family, with a curve in the middle. Elbow macaroni is usually eaten with sauces based on meat, sausages and tomato. The closest substitutes for elbow macaroni are straight macaroni (page 7), cotelli or garganelli.

FRICELLI: These small tubes of pasta are formed into pretty spirals. They are not always readily available, but you can substitute cavatelli, penne (page 7), fusilli or garganelli.

FUSILLI: This corkscrew-shaped pasta can range in size from 4 to 30 cm (1½ to 12 inch) long; we have used pieces that are about 4 cm (1½ inch). Fusilli is most often available in dried form. It is commonly served with meat dishes and simple tomato sauces. You can replace fusilli with farfalle, penne (page 7), cotelli or garganelli.

GARGANELLI: This pasta is made with an egg dough that has grated Parmesan and nutmeg added to it. The outside surface of garganelli is ribbed. The ribs are formed by cutting the pasta into 4 cm (1½ inch) squares, wrapping the squares around a conical tool, then pressing them onto a ribbed wooden block. Garganelli is commonly served in a broth or with Bolognese sauce but is suitable for a wide range of pasta sauces. Penne (page 7), fricelli or fusilli can all be substituted for garganelli.

COTELLI WITH SPRING VEGETABLES

Preparation time: 15 minutes
Cooking time: 20 minutes
Serves 4

500 g (1 lb 2 oz) cotelli
310 g (2 cups) frozen peas
310 g (2 cups) frozen broad (fava) beans, blanched and peeled
80 ml (1/3 cup) olive oil
6 spring onions (scallions), cut into 3 cm (1 1/4 inch) pieces
2 garlic cloves, finely chopped
250 ml (1 cup) chicken stock, preferably home-made
12 thin fresh asparagus spears, cut into 5 cm (2 inch) lengths
1 lemon

1 Cook the pasta in a large saucepan of boiling water until *al dente*. Drain, then return to the pan. Meanwhile, place the peas in a saucepan of boiling water and cook them for 1–2 minutes, or until tender. Remove with a slotted spoon and plunge into cold water. Add the broad beans to the same saucepan of boiling water and cook for 1–2 minutes, then drain and plunge into cold water. Remove and slip the skins off.

2 Heat 2 tablespoons of the oil in a frying pan. Add the spring onion and garlic and cook over medium heat for 2 minutes, or until softened. Pour in the stock and cook for 5 minutes, or until slightly reduced. Add the asparagus and cook for 3–4 minutes, or until bright green and just tender. Stir in the peas and broad beans and cook for 2–3 minutes, or until heated through.

3 Toss the remaining oil through the pasta, then add the vegetable mixture, 1/2 teaspoon finely grated lemon rind and 60 ml (1/4 cup) lemon juice. Season and toss together well. Divide among four bowls and top with shaved Parmesan, if desired.

NUTRITION PER SERVE
Fat 20.5 g; Protein 24.5 g; Carbohydrate 102.5 g; Dietary Fibre 18.5 g; Cholesterol 0 mg; 2935 kJ (700 Cal)

RICH CHEESE MACARONI

Preparation time: 15 minutes
Cooking time: 40 minutes
Serves 4

450 g (1 lb) elbow macaroni
40 g (1½ oz) butter
300 ml (10½ fl oz) cream
125 g (4½ oz) fontina cheese, sliced
125 g (4½ oz) provolone cheese, grated
100 g (3½ oz) Gruyère cheese, grated
125 g (4½ oz) blue castello cheese, crumbled
40 g (½ cup) fresh white breadcrumbs
25 g (¼ cup) grated Parmesan cheese

1 Preheat the oven to 180°C (350°F/ Gas 4). Cook the pasta in a large saucepan of boiling water until *al dente*. Drain and keep warm. Melt half the butter in a large saucepan. Add the cream and, when just coming to the boil, add the fontina, provolone, Gruyère and blue castello cheeses, stirring constantly over low heat for 3 minutes, or until melted. Season with salt and ground white pepper. Add the pasta to the cheese mixture and mix well.

2 Spoon the mixture into a lightly greased shallow 2 litre (8 cup) ovenproof dish. Sprinkle with the breadcrumbs mixed with the Parmesan, dot with the remaining cubed butter and bake for 25 minutes, or until the top is golden and crisp. Serve with a salad.

NUTRITION PER SERVE
Fat 81 g; Protein 48.5 g; Carbohydrate 88.5 g; Dietary Fibre 6 g; Cholesterol 260 mg; 5330 kJ (1275 Cal)

1

2

FRICELLI WITH MUSHROOMS AND ROCKET

Preparation time: 15 minutes +
  10 minutes soaking
Cooking time: 15 minutes
Serves 4

10 g (¼ oz) dried porcini mushrooms
375 g (13 oz) fricelli
25 g (1 oz) butter
60 ml (¼ cup) extra virgin olive oil
2 garlic cloves, crushed
250 g (9 oz) button mushrooms, sliced
60 ml (¼ cup) lemon juice
35 g (⅓ cup) grated Parmesan
  cheese
80 g (2¾ oz) baby rocket (arugula)
  leaves, trimmed

1 Soak the porcini in 80 ml (⅓ cup) boiling water for 10 minutes, or until softened. Cook the pasta in a large saucepan of boiling water until *al dente*. Drain and return to the pan.
2 Meanwhile, heat the butter and oil over medium heat in a frying pan. Add the garlic and button mushrooms and cook for 4 minutes, tossing occasionally. Drain the porcini, reserving the soaking liquid. Chop all of the mushrooms, then add to the frying pan with the reserved soaking liquid. Bring to a simmer.
3 Add the mushroom mixture, lemon juice and Parmesan to the saucepan with the pasta and toss together. Season to taste with salt and ground black pepper. Toss through the rocket just before serving. Spoon into warm serving bowls and serve.

NUTRITION PER SERVE
Fat 22.5 g; Protein 16 g; Carbohydrate 68 g; Dietary Fibre 7 g; Cholesterol 22 mg; 2265 kJ (540 Cal)

1

2

3

COTELLI WITH CAPERS, BOCCONCINI AND BASIL OIL

Preparation time: 10 minutes
Cooking time: 15 minutes
Serves 4–6

125 ml (1/2 cup) olive oil
125 g (4 1/2 oz) jar capers in brine, drained
500 g (1 lb 2 oz) cotelli
2 tablespoons lemon juice
100 g (2 cups) firmly packed fresh basil

35 g (1/3 cup) grated Parmesan cheese
250 g (9 oz) cherry tomatoes, quartered
8 bocconcini cheese, quartered
extra virgin olive oil, for drizzling

1 Heat half the olive oil in a small pan, cook the capers over high heat for 3–4 minutes, or until crisp and golden. Drain on paper towels.
2 Cook the pasta in a large saucepan of boiling water until *al dente*. Drain and keep warm. Meanwhile, place the lemon juice, 75 g (1 1/2 cups) of the basil and the remaining olive oil in a food processor and process until smooth. Season with salt and pepper.
3 Roughly tear the remaining basil leaves, then toss through the warm pasta with the basil mixture, 2 tablespoons of the Parmesan and the cherry tomatoes. Spoon into warmed bowls and top with the bocconcini and capers. Drizzle with extra virgin olive oil and garnish with the remaining grated Parmesan. Serve immediately.

NUTRITION PER SERVE (6)
Fat 26 g; Protein 21 g; Carbohydrate 61 g; Dietary Fibre 5.5 g; Cholesterol 23.5 mg; 2375 kJ (565 Cal)

SPEEDY GOULASH WITH FUSILLI

Preparation time: 15 minutes
Cooking time: 20 minutes
Serves 4

400 g (14 oz) fusilli
2 tablespoons olive oil
1 large onion, sliced into thin wedges
600 g (1 lb 5 oz) rump steak, trimmed and cut into 2 cm (3/4 inch) cubes
1 tablespoon plain (all-purpose) flour
1 small green capsicum (pepper), diced
2 x 425 g (15 oz) cans diced tomatoes (see Note)
1 teaspoon hot paprika
80 g (1/3 cup) light sour cream

1 Cook the pasta in a large saucepan of boiling water until *al dente*. Meanwhile, heat 1 tablespoon of the olive oil in a large frying pan, add the onion and cook, stirring, over medium heat for 4–5 minutes, or until softened and golden. Remove the onion from the pan.

2 Heat the remaining olive oil in the same pan. Toss the steak cubes in the flour, shaking off any excess, then add to the hot pan and cook for 2 minutes over high heat to brown on all sides. Add the capsicum, tomato, paprika and the cooked onion and stir to combine.

3 Bring the mixture to the boil, then reduce the heat and simmer for 8–10 minutes, stirring occasionally. Season with salt and ground black pepper. To serve, place the fusilli in serving bowls, spoon on the goulash mixture and top each serving with a tablespoon of sour cream.

NUTRITION PER SERVE
Fat 18.5 g; Protein 49.5 g; Carbohydrate 81.5 g; Dietary Fibre 8 g; Cholesterol 113 mg; 2925 kJ (700 Cal)

COOK'S FILE
Note: We used cans of tomatoes that are spiced with garlic and black pepper—they really added depth to the flavour of our goulash.

1

2

3

CRESTI DI GALLO WITH CREAMY TOMATO AND BACON SAUCE

Preparation time: 10 minutes
Cooking time: 15 minutes
Serves 4

400 g (14 oz) cresti di gallo
1 tablespoon olive oil
170 g (6 oz) streaky bacon, thinly sliced (see Note)
500 g (1 lb 2 oz) Roma (plum) tomatoes, roughly chopped
125 ml (1/2 cup) thick (double/heavy) cream
2 tablespoons sun-dried (sun-blushed) tomato pesto
2 tablespoons finely chopped fresh flat-leaf (Italian) parsley
50 g (1/2 cup) finely grated Parmesan cheese

1 Cook the pasta in a large saucepan of boiling water until *al dente*. Drain and return to the pan. Meanwhile, heat the oil in a frying pan, add the bacon and cook over high heat for 2 minutes, or until starting to brown. Reduce the heat to medium, add the tomato and cook, stirring frequently, for 2 minutes, or until the tomato has softened but still holds its shape.
2 Stir in the cream and pesto until heated through. Remove from heat, add the parsley, then toss the sauce and Parmesan through the pasta.

NUTRITION PER SERVE
Fat 28.5 g; Protein 24.5 g; Carbohydrate 75 g; Dietary Fibre 7 g; Cholesterol 62.5 mg; 2745 kJ (655 Cal)

COOK'S FILE
Note: Streaky bacon is the tail end of bacon rashers. It is fattier but adds to the flavour of the meal. You can use 170 g (6 oz) bacon rashers if you prefer.

1

2

WARM SWEET POTATO, ROCKET AND WALNUT SALAD

Preparation time: 15 minutes
Cooking time: 30 minutes
Serves 4

800 g (1 lb 12 oz) orange sweet
    potato, cut into 2 cm (³/4 inch)
    cubes
150 ml (5 fl oz) olive oil
125 g (1 cup) walnut pieces
350 g (12 oz) fricelli
150 g (5¹/2 oz) white castello cheese,
    softened
2 garlic cloves, crushed
2 teaspoons lemon juice
¹/2 teaspoon sugar
100 g (3¹/2 oz) baby rocket (arugula)
    or baby spinach leaves

1 Preheat the oven to 200°C (400°F/ Gas 6). Toss the orange sweet potato in 2 tablespoons of the oil and place in a single layer on a baking tray lined with baking paper. Season. Cook, turning halfway through, for 30 minutes, or until golden and cooked through. Spread the walnuts onto a separate baking tray and place in the oven for the last 10 minutes, or until crisp and golden.
2 Meanwhile, cook the pasta in a large saucepan of boiling water until *al dente*. Drain, then return to the pan. Remove the rind from one third of the cheese and cut the rest into cubes. Finely chop 2 tablespoons of the toasted walnuts and place in a jar with the garlic, lemon juice, sugar, remaining oil and rindless cheese and season. Shake the jar until well combined. You may need to break the cheese up with a fork to help mix it through if it is too firm.
3 Toss the pasta, sweet potato, rocket, cubed cheese and remaining walnuts in a bowl, drizzle with the dressing and toss together. Divide among four serving bowls and season to taste with salt and black pepper.

NUTRITION PER SERVE
Fat 69 g; Protein 26.5 g; Carbohydrate 91.5 g;
Dietary Fibre 11 g; Cholesterol 37.5 mg;
4570 kJ (1090 Cal)

CHICKEN, BROCCOLI AND PASTA BAKE

Preparation time: 15 minutes
Cooking time: 35 minutes
Serves 6–8

300 g (10^1/$_2$ oz) fusilli
425 g (15 oz) can cream of
  mushroom soup
2 eggs
185 g (^{3}/$_4$ cup) whole-egg mayonnaise
1 tablespoon Dijon mustard
210 g (1^2/$_3$ cups) grated Cheddar
  cheese

600 g (1 lb 5 oz) chicken breast fillets,
  thinly sliced
400 g (14 oz) frozen broccoli pieces,
  thawed
40 g (^{1}/$_2$ cup) fresh breadcrumbs

1 Preheat the oven to 180°C (350°/
Gas 4). Cook the pasta in a large
saucepan of boiling water until
al dente, then drain and return to the
pan. Combine the soup, eggs,
mayonnaise, mustard and half the
cheese in a bowl.
2 Heat a lightly greased non-stick
frying pan over medium heat, add
the chicken pieces and cook for

5–6 minutes, or until cooked
through. Season with salt and
pepper, then set aside to cool.
3 Add the chicken and broccoli to
the pasta, pour the soup mixture
over the top and stir until well
combined. Transfer the mixture to
a 3 litre (12 cup) ovenproof dish.
Sprinkle with the combined
breadcrumbs and remaining cheese.
Bake for 20 minutes, or until the top
becomes golden brown.

NUTRITION PER SERVE (8)
Fat 32.5 g; Protein 33.5 g; Carbohydrate 33 g;
Dietary Fibre 4.5 g; Cholesterol 143 mg;
2340 kJ (560 Cal)

1

2

3

WARM LAMB, PASTA AND CHARGRILLED CAPSICUM SALAD

Preparation time: 15 minutes +
   10 minutes standing
Cooking time: 30 minutes
Serves 6

125 ml (½ cup) olive oil
1 tablespoon chopped fresh rosemary
2 garlic cloves, crushed
400 g (14 oz) lamb fillets (backstrap)
60 g (¼ cup) wholegrain mustard
400 g (14 oz) fricelli
250 g (9 oz) snow peas (mangetout), trimmed
320 g (2 cups) ready-made chargrilled, skinned red capsicum (pepper), thinly sliced (see Note)
100 g (3½ oz) Swiss cheese, shaved

1 Preheat the oven to 190°C (375°F/ Gas 5). Place the oil, rosemary and garlic in a frying pan and cook, stirring, over low heat for 2 minutes, or until fragrant and lightly golden. Strain the oil into a large bowl, then return half of it to the pan. Add the rosemary and garlic to the bowl. Reheat the frying pan over high heat, add the lamb; cook for 30 seconds each side, or until browned. Transfer the lamb to a baking dish and roast for 8 minutes; rest for 10 minutes.
2 Pour any remaining oil from the frying pan and any juices from the baking dish into the bowl with the rosemary and garlic. Add the mustard and stir together well. While the meat rests, cook the pasta in a large saucepan of boiling water until *al dente*. Drain and transfer to the bowl with the oil mixture. Bring a

saucepan of water to the boil, add the snow peas and cook for 30 seconds, then drain and set aside.
3 Thinly slice the lamb on the diagonal and place in the bowl with the pasta. Add the snow peas, capsicum and two thirds of the cheese. Season with salt and pepper. Toss together well. Divide among four serving plates or bowls and sprinkle with the remaining cheese.

NUTRITION PER SERVE
Fat 21 g; Protein 29.5 g; Carbohydrate 51.5 g; Dietary Fibre 5.5 g; Cholesterol 59.5 mg; 2150 kJ (515 Cal)

COOK'S FILE
Note: You can buy chargrilled capsicum from the deli section of some of the big supermarkets. Alternatively, use a well-drained jar of chargrilled capsicum.

CRAB, CAMEMBERT AND FUSILLI FRITTATA

Preparation time: 15 minutes
Cooking time: 50 minutes
Serves 4–6

80 g (1 cup) tri-coloured fusilli
1 tablespoon olive oil
1 very small red onion, finely chopped
1 large Roma (plum) tomato, roughly chopped
60 g (1/3 cup) semi-dried (sun-blushed) tomatoes, roughly chopped
2 tablespoons finely chopped fresh coriander (cilantro) leaves
140 g (2/3 cup) cooked fresh or canned crab meat
150 g (5 1/2 oz) Camembert cheese, rind removed, cut into small pieces
6 eggs plus 2 egg yolks

1 Cook the pasta in a large saucepan of boiling water until *al dente*. Drain, rinse, then drain again and set aside to cool. Meanwhile, heat half the oil in a small frying pan over low heat, add the onion and cook for 4–5 minutes, or until softened but not browned. Transfer to a bowl and add the Roma tomato, semi-dried tomatoes and coriander. Squeeze out any excess moisture from the crab meat and add the meat to the bowl. Add half the cheese to the bowl, then add the cooled pasta. Mix well. Beat together the six eggs and the two extra yolks, then stir into the tomato and crab mixture. Season.

2 Heat the remaining oil in the frying pan, pour in the frittata mixture and cook over low heat for 25 minutes. Preheat the grill (broiler) to low. Scatter the remaining Camembert over the frittata before placing it under the grill for 10–15 minutes, or until cooked and golden brown on top. Remove from the grill and leave for 5 minutes. Cut into slices and serve with salad and bread.

NUTRITION PER SERVE (6)
Fat 17 g; Protein 18.5 g; Carbohydrate 12.5 g; Dietary Fibre 2 g; Cholesterol 293 mg; 1155 kJ (275 Cal)

PEPPERED PORK, ZUCCHINI AND GARGANELLI

Preparation time: 15 minutes
Cooking time: 25 minutes
Serves 4

450 g (1 lb) pork fillet
3–4 teaspoons cracked black
    peppercorns
80 g (2¾ oz) butter
250 g (9 oz) garganelli
1 onion, halved and thinly sliced
2 large zucchini (courgettes), thinly
    sliced
20 g (⅔ cup) fresh basil, torn
155 g (¾ cup) baby black olives
60 g (½ cup) grated Romano cheese

1 Cut the pork fillet in half widthways and roll in the pepper and some salt. Heat half the butter in a large deep frying pan, add the pork and cook for 4 minutes each side, or until golden brown and just cooked through. Remove from the pan and cut into 5 mm (¼ inch) slices, then set aside and keep warm.

2 Cook the pasta in a large saucepan of boiling water until *al dente*; drain well and return to the pan. Meanwhile, melt the remaining butter in the frying pan, add the onion and cook, stirring, over medium heat for about 3 minutes, or until soft. Add the zucchini and toss for 5 minutes, or until starting to soften. Add the basil, olives, sliced pork and any juices and toss well. Stir the pork mixture through the hot pasta, then season to taste with salt and ground black pepper. Serve immediately, topped with the cheese.

NUTRITION PER SERVE
Fat 21.5 g; Protein 38.5 g; Carbohydrate 52.5 g; Dietary Fibre 5 g; Cholesterol 113.5 mg; 2340 kJ (560 Cal)

CREAMY PORK AND APPLE WITH FRICELLI

Preparation time: 15 minutes
Cooking time: 25 minutes
Serves 4

375 g (13 oz) fricelli
60 g (2¼ oz) butter
2 Granny Smith apples, peeled, cored and cut into thin wedges
2 pork fillets (500 g/1 lb 2 oz in total), thinly sliced
375 ml (1½ cups) chicken stock
250 ml (1 cup) dry alcoholic cider
3 teaspoons wholegrain mustard
2 garlic cloves, crushed
170 ml (⅔ cup) thick (double/heavy) cream

1 Cook the pasta in a large saucepan of boiling water until *al dente*. Drain, cover and set aside to keep warm. Meanwhile, heat 20 g (½ oz) of the butter in a large frying pan, add the apple and cook over high heat, turning occasionally, for 4 minutes until golden. Remove from the pan, cover and keep warm. Add 20 g (½ oz) butter to the same pan and stir-fry half the pork for 2–3 minutes, or until seared and just browned. Remove from the pan and keep warm. Repeat with the remaining butter and pork.

2 Add the stock, cider, mustard and garlic to the pan and boil for about 10 minutes, or until the sauce has reduced by half, scraping up any sediment with a wooden spoon.

Reduce the heat to medium and add the cream, pork and any cooking juices and cook for 2–3 minutes, or until the pork is just cooked through and tender.

3 Stir in two thirds of the apple, being careful not to break it up, then mix in the pasta. Serve topped with a few pieces of the remaining apple.

NUTRITION PER SERVE
Fat 30 g; Protein 40 g; Carbohydrate 78.5 g; Dietary Fibre 6.5 g; Cholesterol 199 mg; 3195 kJ (765 Cal)

COOK'S FILE
Note: Don't use a non-stick frying pan to cook the apples because they will not caramelize properly.

WARM MINTED CHICKEN AND PASTA SALAD

Preparation time: 15 minutes
Cooking time: 20 minutes
Serves 4

250 g (9 oz) cotelli
125 ml (1/2 cup) olive oil
1 large red capsicum (pepper)
3 chicken breast fillets
6 spring onions (scallions), cut into
   2 cm (3/4 inch) lengths
4 garlic cloves, thinly sliced
35 g (3/4 cup) chopped fresh mint
80 ml (1/3 cup) cider vinegar
100 g (31/2 oz) baby spinach leaves

1 Cook the pasta in a large saucepan of boiling water until *al dente*, drain, stir in 1 tablespoon of the oil and set aside. Meanwhile, cut the capsicum into quarters, removing the seeds and membrane. Place, skin-side-up, under a hot grill for 8–10 minutes, or until the skin blackens and blisters. Cool in a plastic bag, then peel away the skin. Cut into thin strips. Place the chicken between two sheets of plastic wrap and press with the palm of your hand until slightly flattened.
2 Heat 1 tablespoon of the oil in a frying pan, cook the chicken over medium heat for 2–3 minutes each side, or until light brown and cooked

through. Remove from the pan and cut into 5 mm (1/4 inch) slices.
3 Add another tablespoon of the oil to the pan and add the spring onion, garlic and capsicum and cook, stirring, for 2–3 minutes, or until starting to soften. Add 25 g (1/2 cup) of the mint, the vinegar and the remaining oil and stir until warmed through. In a large bowl, combine the pasta, chicken, spinach, onion mixture and remaining mint and toss well, seasoning to taste. Serve warm.

NUTRITION PER SERVE
Fat 30 g; Protein 47 g; Carbohydrate 46.5 g; Dietary Fibre 5.5 g; Cholesterol 84 mg; 2705 kJ (645 Cal)

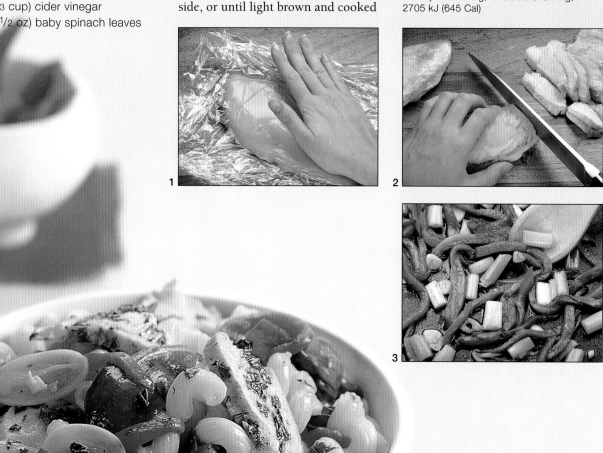

COTELLI, TOMATO AND ARTICHOKE GRILL

Preparation time: 15 minutes
Cooking time: 20 minutes
Serves 4

350 g (12 oz) cotelli
285 g (10 oz) jar marinated artichoke
    hearts, drained and chopped
2 tablespoons olive oil
250 ml (1 cup) thick (double/heavy)
    cream

2 tablespoons chopped fresh thyme
2 garlic cloves, crushed
75 g ($^3/_4$ cup) grated Parmesan
    cheese
210 g (1$^2/_3$ cups) grated Cheddar
    cheese
950 g (2 lb 2 oz) tomatoes, cut into
    5 mm ($^1/_4$ inch) slices

1 Cook the pasta in a large saucepan of boiling water until *al dente*. Drain; return to the pan. Grease a 23 cm x 30 cm (9 inch x 12 inch) rectangular ovenproof dish. Stir the artichokes,

olive oil, cream, thyme, garlic, half the Parmesan and 155 g (1$^1/_4$ cups) of the Cheddar through the pasta and season. Spread evenly in the dish.
2 Arrange the tomatoes over the top, overlapping one another. Season, then sprinkle with the remaining cheese. Cook under a hot grill (broiler) for 6 minutes, or until the cheeses melt and are golden brown.

NUTRITION PER SERVE
Fat 55.5 g; Protein 33 g; Carbohydrate 69 g; Dietary Fibre 9 g; Cholesterol 137 mg; 3800 kJ (910 Cal)

ANGEL HAIR PASTA

BUCATINI

FETTUCINE

LINGUINE

SPAGHETTI

SPAGHETTINI

TAGLIATELLE

VERMICELLI

ZITI

LONG

Fresh or dried, long pasta may not be the tidiest of meals, but the sensation of eating the thin strands makes it all worthwhile.

ANGEL HAIR PASTA: Also called capelli d'angelo, this pasta is only available in dried form and it is the thinnest of all the spaghetti pastas. Resembling strands of long, blonde hair, its fine texture is best suited for use in broths and with extremely delicate, light, smooth sauces. Angel hair pasta can be replaced with capellini (not shown), spaghettini or vermicelli.

BUCATINI: Similar to thick spaghetti but with a hollow centre that helps it cook more quickly than spaghetti. Bucatini means small hole in Italian. It is traditionally served with carbonara and Amatriciana sauces. You can substitute linguine, spaghetti or one of the longer fusilli pastas (page 31) for bucatini.

FETTUCINE: This pasta is slightly narrower and thicker than the very similar pasta, tagliatelle. It is usually served with rich, creamy sauces or simple fresh flavours, because the thickness of the strands helps it to carry the accompanying sauce. You can use trenette (not shown) or tagliatelle instead. There are several varieties of this very popular pasta; we have used only a few of the many types available.
Fresh spinach fettucine: Also known as *fettucine verde* due to its rich green colour, it is made by the addition of cooked, well-drained spinach to the dough before it is kneaded. The most popular of the coloured pastas, its colour makes it an attractive companion to both red tomato-based sauces and white cream-based ones.
Fresh basil fettucine: While it is uncommon to find herbs in pasta as they are usually included in the sauce, there are some regional specialities which incorporate finely chopped herbs, such as basil, in the pasta dough. When using a herb-flavoured pasta, choose simple sauces whose flavours won't compete with or overshadow the flavour of the pasta. These speciality pastas are usually only available home-made or in pasta shops.

LINGUINE (fresh, dried): The Italian word for 'little tongues', linguine is a long flat pasta also known as bavette. It is good with pesto or seafood sauces. Substitute bucatini, fettucine, spaghetti, tagliatelle or long fusilli (page 31), remembering that if the recipe asks for fresh pasta, use fresh and if it asks for dried, use dried.

SPAGHETTI (fresh, dried): The name of this very popular pasta comes from the Italian word 'strings'. Nowadays, spaghetti is made all over the world. The commercial making of spaghetti involves pushing the pasta dough through an extrusion system to make the noodles. Out of all the hundreds of pasta shapes, spaghetti is the most versatile. It is suitable for a large number of sauces and it comes in 2–3 different thicknesses, one being thin spaghetti, also known as spaghettini. Substitute bucatini or spaghettini. Always replace fresh pasta with fresh and dried pasta with dried.

SPAGHETTINI: Very similar to spaghetti, but even thinner, these so-called 'little lengths of cord' make an ideal match for delicate, oil-based sauces such as the Italian classic aglio e olio (garlic and olive oil) or fish and shellfish sauces. Spaghettini is often only available as dried pasta. Substitute other long, fine pastas such as angel hair pasta, spaghetti or vermicelli.

TAGLIATELLE (fresh, dried): Slightly wider than fettucine, these very thin, flat ribbon noodles are the northern Italian name for fettucine. In fact, the two are interchangeable. Tagliatelle, *not* spaghetti, is the traditional accompaniment to Bolognese sauce. Unlike other pasta shapes, both fresh and dried tagliatelle are made with the addition of egg to the pasta dough. Like other ribbon pastas, it is at its best when accompanied by light cream or butter-based sauces, or fresh flavours. You can substitute lasagnette (page 91) or fettucine.

VERMICELLI: Meaning 'little worms' in Italian, it is a very fine, long pasta best eaten in broth-based noodle soups or with fine-textured tomato, butter or cheese sauces which cling well to its length. Vermicelli is thinner than spaghetti. Replace with spaghettini or angel hair pasta.

ZITI: A long, tubular pasta, its strong, thick texture and hollow interior are excellent for picking up heavy meat sauces such as ragus and chunky vegetable sauces. Unlike other long pastas, it is often broken into smaller pieces prior to cooking. It can be replaced with pasta of a similar size like candele (not shown), lasagnette (page 91), rigatoni, penne (page 7) or bucatini.

SPAGHETTI BOLOGNESE

Preparation time: 10 minutes
Cooking time: 55 minutes
Serves 4

1 tablespoon olive oil
1 large onion, diced
2 garlic cloves, crushed
600 g (1 lb 5 oz) minced (ground)
    beef (or minced beef and veal)
125 ml (1/2 cup) red wine
125 ml (1/2 cup) beef stock
2 x 400 g (14 oz) cans chopped
    tomatoes
1 carrot, grated
350 g (12 oz) spaghetti

1 Heat the oil over medium heat in a large saucepan, add the onion and garlic and cook for 1–2 minutes, or until soft. Add the meat and cook, stirring to break up any lumps, for 5 minutes, or until the meat is browned. Pour in the wine and simmer for 2–3 minutes, or until reduced slightly, then add the stock and simmer for 2 minutes. Add the tomato and carrot and season well. Cook over low heat for 40 minutes.
2 About 15 minutes before serving, cook the pasta in a large saucepan of boiling water until *al dente*. Drain well and keep warm. Divide the pasta evenly among four serving bowls and pour the meat sauce over the pasta. Garnish with parsley, if desired.

NUTRITION PER SERVE
Fat 22.5 g; Protein 42.5 g; Carbohydrate 70.5 g; Dietary Fibre 8 g; Cholesterol 94.5 mg; 2830 kJ (675 Cal)

COOK'S FILE
Hint: Delicious with grated Parmesan cheese.

1

2

BUCATINI WITH SAUSAGE AND FENNEL SEED

Preparation time: 10 minutes
Cooking time: 40 minutes
Serves 4

500 g (1 lb 2 oz) good-quality Italian sausages
2 tablespoons olive oil
3 garlic cloves, chopped
1 teaspoon fennel seeds
1/2 teaspoon chilli flakes
2 x 425 g (15 oz) cans crushed tomatoes
500 g (1 lb 2 oz) bucatini
1 teaspoon balsamic vinegar
7 g (1/4 cup) loosely packed fresh basil, chopped

1 Heat a frying pan over high heat, add the sausages and cook, turning, for 8–10 minutes, or until well browned and cooked through. Remove, cool slightly and slice on the diagonal into 1 cm (1/2 inch) pieces.
2 Heat the oil in a saucepan, add the garlic and cook over medium heat for 1 minute. Add the fennel seeds and chilli flakes and cook for 1 minute. Stir in the tomato and bring to the boil, then reduce the heat and simmer, covered, for 20 minutes. Cook the pasta in a large saucepan of boiling water until *al dente*. Drain. Return to the pan to keep warm.
3 Add the sausages to the sauce and cook, uncovered, for 5 minutes to heat through. Stir in the vinegar and basil. Divide the pasta among four bowls, top with the sauce and serve.

NUTRITION PER SERVE
Fat 50.5 g; Protein 34 g; Carbohydrate 96 g; Dietary Fibre 9.5 g; Cholesterol 95 mg; 4125 kJ (985 Cal)

1

2

3

LINGUINE WITH HAM, ARTICHOKE AND LEMON SAUCE

Preparation time: 15 minutes
Cooking time: 10 minutes
Serves 4

500 g (1 lb 2 oz) fresh linguine
25 g (1 oz) butter
2 large garlic cloves, chopped
150 g (5½ oz) marinated artichokes, drained and quartered
150 g (5½ oz) sliced leg ham, cut into strips
300 ml (10½ fl oz) cream
2 teaspoons coarsely grated lemon zest
15 g (½ cup) fresh basil, torn
35 g (⅓ cup) grated Parmesan cheese

1 Cook the pasta in a large saucepan of boiling water until *al dente*. Drain, then return to the pan. Meanwhile, melt the butter in a large frying pan, add the garlic and cook over medium heat for 1 minute, or until fragrant. Add the artichokes and ham and cook for a further 2 minutes.

2 Add the cream and lemon zest, reduce the heat and simmer for 5 minutes, gently breaking up the artichokes with a spoon. Pour the sauce over the pasta, then add the basil and Parmesan and toss until the pasta is evenly coated. Divide among four serving plates and serve.

NUTRITION PER SERVE
Fat 42 g; Protein 25.5 g; Carbohydrate 90.5 g; Dietary Fibre 7.5 g; Cholesterol 143 mg; 3540 kJ (845 Cal)

FRESH FETTUCINE WITH BALSAMIC SEARED TUNA CHUNKS

Preparation time: 15 minutes +
  10 minutes marinating
Cooking time: 15 minutes
Serves 4–6

4 x 200 g (7 oz) tuna steaks
170 ml ($2/3$ cup) balsamic vinegar
125 ml ($1/2$ cup) good-quality olive oil
1 lemon
1 garlic clove, finely chopped
1 red onion, finely chopped
2 tablespoons capers, rinsed and dried
10 g ($1/2$ cup) fresh flat-leaf (Italian)
  parsley, finely chopped
500 g (1 lb 2 oz) fresh fettucine

1 Place the tuna in a non-metallic dish and cover with the balsamic vinegar. Turn to coat evenly with the vinegar and marinate for 10 minutes. Heat 2 tablespoons of the oil in a large frying pan over medium heat and cook the tuna steaks for 2–3 minutes each side. Remove from the pan, cut into 2 cm ($3/4$ inch) cubes and transfer to a bowl.

2 Finely grate the rind from the lemon to give $1/2$ teaspoon zest, then squeeze the lemon to give 60 ml ($1/4$ cup) juice. Wipe the frying pan clean, and heat 2 tablespoons of the olive oil over medium heat, then add the garlic and cook for 30 seconds. Stir in the chopped onion and cook for 2 minutes. Add the lemon zest and capers and cook for 1 minute,

then stir in the parsley and cook for 1 minute. Add the lemon juice and remaining oil and gently toss together. Season to taste.

3 Meanwhile, cook the pasta in a large saucepan of boiling water until *al dente*. Drain well, return to the pan and toss the caper mixture through. Divide the pasta among serving bowls and arrange the tuna pieces over the top.

NUTRITION PER SERVE (6)
Fat 26 g; Protein 43 g; Carbohydrate 60 g; Dietary Fibre 4.5 g; Cholesterol 48 mg; 2740 kJ (655 Cal)

TAGLIATELLE WITH SALMON ROE AND HERB BREADCRUMBS

Preparation time: 15 minutes
Cooking time: 20 minutes
Serves 6

8 slices white bread
250 g (9 oz) mascarpone
2 egg yolks
4 garlic cloves
200 ml (7 fl oz) olive oil
500 g (1 lb 2 oz) fresh tagliatelle
3 tablespoons chopped fresh dill
100 g (3½ oz) Parmesan, grated
60 g (2¼ oz) salmon roe

1 Place the slices of bread in a food processor or blender and process until fine breadcrumbs form. Remove from the food processor. Place the mascarpone, egg yolks and 1 clove chopped garlic in the food processor or blender and process until smooth. With the motor running, gradually add half the oil in a thin stream.

2 Cook the pasta in a large saucepan of boiling water until *al dente*, then drain. Meanwhile, heat the remaining oil in a heavy-based frying pan and cook the remaining garlic cloves over medium heat for 2–3 minutes, or until golden brown. Remove the cloves from the oil and discard. Add the fresh breadcrumbs to the warm oil and cook over low heat for 15 minutes, or until golden and crunchy. Remove from the pan and drain on paper towels. When cool, stir in the dill and season lightly with salt and ground black pepper.

3 Add the mascarpone mixture and the Parmesan to the pasta and toss together well. Divide among six serving plates, sprinkle with the breadcrumbs, top with the salmon roe and serve immediately.

NUTRITION PER SERVE
Fat 54 g; Protein 25.5 g; Carbohydrate 77.5 g; Dietary Fibre 5.5 g; Cholesterol 151.5 mg; 3745 kJ (895 Cal)

1

2

3

SPAGHETTI WITH HERB, GARLIC AND CHILLI OIL

Preparation time: 15 minutes
Cooking time: 15 minutes
Serves 4–6

250 ml (1 cup) good-quality olive oil
2 bird's eye chillies, seeded and thinly
    sliced
5–6 large cloves garlic, crushed
500 g (1 lb 2 oz) spaghetti
100 g (3½ oz) thinly sliced prosciutto
30 g (½ cup) chopped fresh flat-leaf
    (Italian) parsley
2 tablespoons chopped fresh basil
2 tablespoons chopped fresh
    oregano
75 g (¾ cup) good-quality grated
    Parmesan cheese

1 Pour the oil into a small saucepan with the chilli and garlic. Slowly heat the oil over low heat for about 12 minutes to infuse the oil with the garlic and chilli. Don't allow the oil to reach smoking point or the garlic will burn and taste bitter.

2 Meanwhile, cook the pasta in a large saucepan of boiling water until *al dente*. Drain well and return to the pan. Lay the prosciutto on a grill (broiler) tray and cook under a hot grill for 2 minutes each side, or until crispy. Cool and break into pieces.

3 Pour the hot oil mixture over the spaghetti and toss well with the prosciutto, fresh herbs and Parmesan. Season to taste.

NUTRITION PER SERVE (6)
Fat 44 g; Protein 17.5 g; Carbohydrate 59.5 g; Dietary Fibre 5.5 g; Cholesterol 20.5 mg; 2945 kJ (705 Cal)

COOK'S FILE
Note: This is a very simple dish, but it relies on good-quality ingredients.

1

3

2

LINGUINE WITH BROCCOLI, PINE NUTS AND LEMON

Preparation time: 15 minutes
Cooking time: 15 minutes
Serves 4–6

500 g (1 lb 2 oz) linguine
600 g (1 lb 5 oz) broccoli, cut into small florets
80 g (1/2 cup) pine nuts
125 ml (1/2 cup) extra virgin olive oil
2 teaspoons finely grated lemon zest
60 ml (1/4 cup) lemon juice
1 teaspoon dried chilli flakes
50 g (1/2 cup) finely grated good-quality Parmesan cheese

1 Cook the pasta in a large saucepan of boiling water until *al dente*. Drain and return to the pan. Meanwhile, bring a saucepan of water to the boil and cook the broccoli for 2 minutes, or until just tender but still bright green. Drain and set aside.
2 Heat a large non-stick frying pan and toast the pine nuts for 2–3 minutes, or until just golden, shaking the pan to prevent them burning. Remove from the pan and roughly chop. Reduce the heat to low, add the oil and lemon zest to the frying pan and gently heat until fragrant. Add the broccoli, chopped nuts, lemon juice and chilli and stir until warmed through. Season. Add to the pasta with the Parmesan and toss to combine. Divide among serving bowls and serve.

NUTRITION PER SERVE (6)
Fat 27 g; Protein 19 g; Carbohydrate 60 g; Dietary Fibre 9 g; Cholesterol 8 mg; 2355 kJ (560 Cal)

1

2

SPAGHETTI NICOISE

Preparation time: 10 minutes
Cooking time: 15 minutes
Serves 4–6

350 g (12 oz) spaghetti
8 quail eggs (or 4 hen eggs)
1 lemon
3 x 185 g (6¼ oz) cans good-quality
    tuna in oil
50 g (⅓ cup) pitted and halved
    Kalamata olives
100 g (3½ oz) semi-dried (sun-
    blushed) tomatoes, cut lengthways

4 anchovy fillets, chopped into small
    pieces
3 tablespoons baby capers, drained
3 tablespoons chopped fresh flat-leaf
    (Italian) parsley

1 Cook the pasta in a large saucepan of boiling water until *al dente*. Meanwhile, place the eggs in a saucepan of cold water, bring to the boil and cook for 4 minutes (10 minutes for hen eggs). Drain, cool under cold water, then peel. Cut the quail eggs into halves or the hen eggs into quarters. Finely grate the rind of the lemon to give 1 teaspoon of grated zest. Then, squeeze the lemon to give 2 tablespoons juice.
2 Empty the tuna and its oil into a large bowl. Add the olives, tomato halves, anchovies, lemon zest and juice, capers and 2 tablespoons of the parsley. Drain the pasta and rinse in a little cold water, then toss gently through the tuna mixture. Divide among serving bowls, garnish with egg and the extra chopped fresh parsley, and serve.

NUTRITION PER SERVE (6)
Fat 26 g; Protein 31.5 g; Carbohydrate 46.5 g; Dietary Fibre 4.5 g; Cholesterol 152.5 mg; 2300 kJ (550 Cal)

1

2

TAGLIATELLE WITH SALMON AND CREAMY DILL DRESSING

Preparation time: 10 minutes
Cooking time: 15 minutes
Serves 4

350 g (12 oz) fresh tagliatelle
60 ml (¼ cup) olive oil
3 x 200 g (7 oz) salmon fillets, skinned and boned (ask your fishmonger to do this for you)
3 garlic cloves, crushed
375 ml (1½ cups) cream

1½ tablespoons chopped fresh dill
1 teaspoon mustard powder
1 tablespoon lemon juice
40 g (1½ oz) shaved Parmesan cheese

1 Cook the pasta in a large saucepan of boiling water until *al dente*. Drain, then toss with 1 tablespoon oil. Meanwhile, heat the remaining oil in a deep frying pan; cook the salmon for 2 minutes each side, or until crisp on the outside but still pink inside. Remove from the pan, cut into 2 cm (¾ inch) cubes; keep warm.
2 In the same pan, add the garlic and cook for 30 seconds, or until fragrant. Add the cream, dill and mustard powder, bring to the boil, then reduce the heat and simmer, stirring, for 4–5 minutes, or until thickened. Season.

3 Add the salmon and any juices plus the lemon juice to the dill sauce and stir until warm. Gently toss the salmon sauce through the pasta and divide among four serving bowls. Sprinkle with Parmesan and serve.

NUTRITION PER SERVE
Fat 66 g; Protein 45 g; Carbohydrate 51 g; Dietary Fibre 1.5 g; Cholesterol 215 mg; 4100 kJ (980 Cal)

SPAGHETTI PRIMAVERA

Preparation time: 15 minutes
Cooking time: 15 minutes
Serves 4

400 g (14 oz) spaghetti
80 ml (¹/₃ cup) extra virgin olive oil
200 g (7 oz) fresh asparagus, trimmed
    and cut into 5 cm (2 inch) lengths
155 g (1 cup) frozen peas
155 g (1 cup) frozen broad (fava) beans
1 leek, thinly sliced
2 tablespoons finely chopped fresh
    flat-leaf (Italian) parsley
250 ml (1 cup) thick (double/heavy)
    cream
35 g (¹/₃ cup) grated Parmesan
    cheese

1 Cook the pasta in a large saucepan of boiling water until *al dente*. Rinse and drain well, then return to the pan, toss with 2 tablespoons of the oil and keep warm.

2 Meanwhile, bring a saucepan of water to the boil and cook the asparagus and peas for 2 minutes, or until bright green and tender. Remove with a slotted spoon and plunge into cold water. Return the pan to the boil and cook the broad beans for 2 minutes, or until tender. Drain, cool, then slip off their skins.

3 Heat the remaining oil in a frying pan and cook the leek over low heat for 2–3 minutes, or until soft but not brown. Add the blanched vegetables and cook for 1 minute, or until warmed through. Stir in the parsley and cream and simmer for 2–3 minutes. Toss the sauce and Parmesan through the pasta, season well and serve.

NUTRITION PER SERVE
Fat 43 g; Protein 21 g; Carbohydrate 77 g;
Dietary Fibre 10.5 g; Cholesterol 78 mg;
3270 kJ (780 Cal)

COOK'S FILE
Note: If fresh broad beans and peas are in season, use them and peel the pods before cooking.

TAGLIATELLE WITH FETA, TOMATO AND ROCKET

Preparation time: 15 minutes
Cooking time: 15 minutes
Serves 4

4 vine-ripened tomatoes
1 small red onion, finely chopped
4 tablespoons shredded fresh
    basil
2 tablespoons olive oil
375 g (13 oz) tagliatelle
2 garlic cloves, finely chopped

150 g (5¹/₂ oz) baby rocket (arugula)
    leaves
150 g (5¹/₂ oz) soft feta cheese,
    crumbled
15 g (¹/₄ cup) fresh small whole
    basil leaves

1 Score a cross in the base of each tomato, then place in a bowl of boiling water for 1 minute. Plunge into cold water and peel the skin away from the cross. Cut in half and remove the seeds with a teaspoon. Chop, then transfer to a bowl. Add the onion and basil, stir in

1 tablespoon of the oil and set aside.
2 Cook the pasta in a large saucepan of boiling water until *al dente*. Drain, reserving 125 ml (¹/₂ cup) pasta water. Return the pasta to the pan, add the remaining oil, the garlic and reserved pasta water, tossing over medium heat for 1–2 minutes until warm. Stir in the tomato mixture, rocket and feta. Season. Divide among four plates and garnish with basil leaves.

NUTRITION PER SERVE
Fat 18 g; Protein 20 g; Carbohydrate 70.5 g;
Dietary Fibre 7.5 g; Cholesterol 26 mg;
2205 kJ (525 Cal)

ANGEL HAIR PASTA WITH SCALLOPS AND ROCKET

Preparation time: 15 minutes
Cooking time: 15 minutes
Serves 4

350 g (12 oz) angel hair pasta
100 g (3½ oz) butter
3 garlic cloves, crushed
24 scallops, without roe
150 g (5½ oz) baby rocket (arugula) leaves
2 teaspoons finely grated lemon zest
60 ml (¼ cup) lemon juice
125 g (4½ oz) semi-dried (sun-blushed) tomatoes, thinly sliced
30 g (1 oz) shaved Parmesan cheese

1 Cook the pasta in a large saucepan of boiling water until *al dente*.

Meanwhile, melt the butter in a small saucepan, add the garlic and cook over low heat, stirring, for 1 minute. Remove from the heat.
2 Heat a lightly greased chargrill plate over high heat and cook the scallops, brushing occasionally with some of the garlic butter for 1–2 minutes each side, or until cooked. Set aside and keep warm.
3 Drain the pasta and return to the pan with the remaining garlic butter, the rocket, lemon zest, lemon juice and tomato and toss until combined. Divide among four serving plates and top with the scallops. Season to taste and sprinkle with Parmesan.

NUTRITION PER SERVE
Fat 25.5 g; Protein 25 g; Carbohydrate 69 g; Dietary Fibre 7.5 g; Cholesterol 97 mg; 2545 kJ (610 Cal)

FETTUCINE WITH CREAMY SPINACH AND ROAST TOMATO

Preparation time: 10 minutes
Cooking time: 35 minutes
Serves 4–6

6 Roma (plum) tomatoes
40 g (1½ oz) butter
2 garlic cloves, crushed
1 onion, chopped
500 g (1 lb 2 oz) English spinach, trimmed
250 ml (1 cup) vegetable stock
125 ml (½ cup) thick (double/heavy) cream
500 g (1 lb 2 oz) fresh spinach fettucine
50 g (1¾ oz) shaved Parmesan cheese

1 Preheat the oven to 220°C (425°F/ Gas 7). Cut the tomatoes in half lengthways, then cut each half into three wedges. Place the wedges on a lightly greased baking tray and bake for 30–35 minutes, or until softened and slightly golden. Meanwhile, heat the butter in a large frying pan. Add the garlic and onion and cook over medium heat for 5 minutes, or until the onion is soft. Add the spinach, stock and cream, increase the heat to high and bring to the boil. Simmer rapidly for 5 minutes.

2 While the spinach mixture is cooking, cook the pasta in a large saucepan of boiling water until *al dente*. Drain and return to the pan. Remove the spinach from the heat and season well. Cool slightly, then process in a food processor until smooth. Toss through the pasta until well coated. Divide among serving bowls, top with the roasted tomatoes and Parmesan shavings.

NUTRITION PER SERVE (6)
Fat 17.5 g; Protein 17 g; Carbohydrate 65 g; Dietary Fibre 7.5 g; Cholesterol 49 mg; 2035 kJ (485 Cal)

SPAGHETTI WITH SMOKED TUNA AND OLIVES

Preparation time: 15 minutes
Cooking time: 20 minutes
Serves 4

800 g (1 lb 12 oz) vine-ripened
    tomatoes
375 g (13 oz) spaghetti
3 x 125 g (4$^{1}/_{2}$ oz) cans smoked tuna
    slices in oil
1 red onion, chopped
2 garlic cloves, crushed
1 teaspoon sugar
150 g (5$^{1}/_{2}$ oz) black olives
2 tablespoons chopped fresh basil
75 g (2$^{1}/_{2}$ oz) Greek feta cheese,
    crumbled

1 Score a cross in the base of each tomato. Place the tomatoes in a bowl of boiling water for 1 minute, then plunge into cold water. Peel the skin away from the cross. Cut in half and remove the seeds with a teaspoon. Roughly chop the flesh. Cook the pasta in a large pan of boiling water until *al dente*. Drain and keep warm.

2 Drain the oil from the tuna slices, reserving 1 tablespoon. Heat the reserved oil in a large saucepan, add the onion and cook over low heat for 3–4 minutes, or until soft but not brown. Add the garlic and cook for another minute, then add the chopped tomatoes and sugar. Cook over medium heat for 8–10 minutes, or until pulpy.

3 Add the tuna slices, olives and chopped basil, stir well and cook for 2 minutes, or until warmed through. Toss through the spaghetti and season. Sprinkle with crumbled feta and serve immediately, accompanied by shaved Parmesan if desired.

NUTRITION PER SERVE
Fat 19 g; Protein 40 g; Carbohydrate 83 g; Dietary Fibre 7.5 g; Cholesterol 50.5 mg; 2795 kJ (670 Cal)

1

2

3

SPAGHETTI MARINARA

Preparation time: 15 minutes
Cooking time: 35 minutes
Serves 4–6

2 tablespoons olive oil
1 onion, finely chopped
2 garlic cloves, crushed
2 x 400 g (14 oz) cans chopped
    tomatoes
1/4 cup (60 g) tomato paste (purée)
500 g (1 lb 2 oz) spaghetti
500 g (1 lb 2 oz) good-quality
    marinara mix (see Note)
8 black mussels, beards removed,
    scrubbed
2 tablespoons shredded fresh basil

1 Heat the oil in a saucepan over medium heat, add the onion and cook for 5 minutes, or until softened and lightly browned. Add the garlic and stir for another 1 minute, or until aromatic. Add the tomato and tomato paste and bring to the boil, then reduce the heat and simmer for 20–25 minutes, or until the sauce becomes rich and pulpy. Stir the sauce occasionally during cooking. Season with salt and ground black pepper. Meanwhile, cook the pasta in a large saucepan of boiling water until *al dente*. Drain well, return to the saucepan and keep warm.
2 Add the marinara mix and the mussels to the tomato sauce and cook for about 2–3 minutes, or until the seafood is cooked and the mussels are open. Discard any mussels that do not open. Stir in the basil. Toss the sauce through the warm pasta and serve.

NUTRITION PER SERVE (6)
Fat 10 g; Protein 34 g; Carbohydrate 68.5 g; Dietary Fibre 6 g; Cholesterol 131 mg; 2125 kJ (510 Cal)

COOK'S FILE
Note: Marinara mix is available from your seafood store. Try to choose a good-quality marinara mix to avoid chewy seafood. Alternatively, you can make your own by choosing a few different types of seafood, such as octopus, fish fillets and calamari and chop into bite-size pieces.

ANGEL HAIR PASTA WITH CREAMY GARLIC PRAWNS

Preparation time: 15 minutes
Cooking time: 15 minutes
Serves 4

2 tablespoons olive oil
16 raw medium prawns (shrimp),
    peeled
1 leek, chopped
6 garlic cloves, crushed
1/2 teaspoon dried chilli flakes
125 ml (1/2 cup) dry white wine
200 ml (7 fl oz) cream
250 g (9 oz) angel hair pasta
3 tablespoons chopped fresh
    flat-leaf (Italian) parsley

1 Heat half the oil in a frying pan and season the prawns. Add to the pan and cook over high heat for 2–3 minutes, or until cooked. Remove from the pan, cover and keep warm.
2 Heat the remaining oil in the same pan, add the leek and cook, stirring, over medium heat for 2–3 minutes, or until softened. Add the garlic and chilli flakes and stir for 1 minute. Pour in the wine, reduce the heat and simmer for 4 minutes, or until reduced. Add the cream and simmer for 3 minutes, or until just thickened.
3 Meanwhile, cook the pasta in a large saucepan of boiling water until *al dente*. Drain and return to the pan. Stir the parsley into the sauce and season well. Add to the pasta and stir to coat. Divide among the serving bowls and top with prawns.

NUTRITION PER SERVE
Fat 32 g; Protein 19.5 g; Carbohydrate 48.5 g; Dietary Fibre 4.5 g; Cholesterol 142.5 mg; 2420 kJ (580 Cal)

1

2

3

1

2

SPAGHETTI WITH SHELLFISH AND WHITE WINE SAUCE

Preparation time: 15 minutes
Cooking time: 10 minutes
Serves 4

500 g (1 lb 2 oz) mussels
1 kg (2 lb 4 oz) clams (vongoles)
400 g (14 oz) fresh spaghetti
2 tablespoons olive oil
4 French shallots, finely chopped
2 garlic cloves, crushed
250 ml (1 cup) dry white wine
3 tablespoons chopped fresh
    flat-leaf (Italian) parsley

1 Scrub the mussels with a stiff brush and remove any barnacles with a knife. Remove the beards. Discard any mussels or clams that are broken or open ones that do not close when tapped on the work surface. Wash them both thoroughly under cold running water. Cook the pasta in a large saucepan of boiling water until *al dente*. Drain and keep warm in a large saucepan.

2 Meanwhile, heat the oil in a large saucepan over medium heat and cook the shallots for 4 minutes, or until softened. Add the garlic and cook for a further 1 minute. Pour in the wine, bring to the boil and cook for 2 minutes, or until reduced slightly. Add the clams and mussels, tossing to coat them in the liquid, then cover the pan. Cook, shaking the pan regularly, for about 3 minutes, or until the shells have opened. Discard any clams or mussels that do not open. Toss the clam mixture through the spaghetti, scatter with parsley and transfer to a warmed serving dish. Season and serve with salad and bread.

NUTRITION PER SERVE
Fat 12 g; Protein 36.5 g; Carbohydrate 75.5 g;
Dietary Fibre 5.5 g; Cholesterol 67.5 mg;
2520 kJ (600 Cal)

FETTUCINE WITH CHERRY TOMATOES, AVOCADO AND BACON

Preparation time: 15 minutes
Cooking time: 25 minutes
Serves 4

4 garlic cloves, unpeeled
80 ml (1/3 cup) olive oil
250 g (9 oz) cherry tomatoes
300 g (10½ oz) short cut bacon
(see Note)
350 g (12 oz) fresh fettucine
1 tablespoon white wine vinegar
2 tablespoons roughly chopped fresh
basil, plus whole leaves to garnish
2 ripe avocados, diced

1 Preheat the oven to 200°C (400°F/ Gas 6). Place the garlic at one end of a roasting tin and drizzle with 2 tablespoons of the olive oil. Place the tomatoes at the other end and season well. Bake for 10 minutes, then remove the garlic. Return the tomatoes to the oven for a further 5–10 minutes, or until soft.

2 Cook the bacon under a hot grill (broiler) for 4–5 minutes each side, or until crisp and golden. Roughly chop. Meanwhile, cook the pasta in a large saucepan of boiling water until *al dente*. Drain well and transfer to a large bowl. Drizzle 1 tablespoon of the olive oil over the pasta and toss well. Season with salt and pepper and keep warm.

3 Slit the skin of each garlic clove and squeeze the garlic out. Place in a screw-top jar with the vinegar, chopped basil and remaining oil and shake well to combine. Add the tomatoes and their juices, bacon and avocado to the fettucine, pour on the dressing and toss well. Garnish with the basil leaves and serve with a green salad and crusty bread.

NUTRITION PER SERVE
Fat 44 g; Protein 27.5 g; Carbohydrate 50.5 g; Dietary Fibre 4 g; Cholesterol 106.5 mg; 2960 kJ (705 Cal)

COOK'S FILE
Note: Short cut bacon is the meaty end of the bacon rasher and is also sold as eye bacon.

FETTUCINE WITH SWEET POTATO, FETA AND OLIVES

Preparation time: 15 minutes
Cooking time: 35 minutes
Serves 6

1.5 kg (3 lb 5 oz) orange sweet potato, cut into 2 cm (3/4 inch) cubes
80 ml (1/3 cup) olive oil
4 garlic cloves, crushed
50 g (1 3/4 oz) butter
4 red onions, sliced into thin wedges
500 g (1 lb 2 oz) fresh basil fettucine

400 g (14 oz) soft feta cheese, cut into 1.5 cm (5/8 inch) cubes
200 g (7 oz) small black olives
30 g (1/2 cup) firmly packed fresh basil, torn

1 Preheat the oven to 200°C (400°F/ Gas 6). Place the sweet potato, oil and garlic in a bowl and toss to coat. Lay out the sweet potato in a roasting tin and roast for 15 minutes, then turn and bake for another 15 minutes, until it is tender and golden—make sure the sweet potato is not too soft or it will not hold its shape. Set aside and keep warm.

2 Meanwhile, melt the butter in a deep frying pan and cook the onion over low heat, stirring occasionally, for 25–30 minutes, or until soft and slightly caramelized.

3 Cook the pasta in a large saucepan of boiling water until *al dente*. Drain and return to the saucepan, then add the onion and toss together. Add the sweet potato, feta, olives and basil and gently toss. Serve drizzled with extra virgin olive oil, if desired.

NUTRITION PER SERVE
Fat 32.5 g; Protein 27.5 g; Carbohydrate 90.5 g; Dietary Fibre 7 g; Cholesterol 124 mg; 3195 kJ (765 Cal)

1

2

3

BAKED BEEF VERMICELLI CAKE

Preparation time: 10 minutes +
  10 minutes standing
Cooking time: 50 minutes
Serves 4–6

80 g (2³/₄ oz) butter
1 onion, chopped
500 g (1 lb 2 oz) minced (ground)
  beef
800 g (1 lb 12 oz) bottled tomato
  pasta sauce
2 tablespoons tomato paste (purée)
250 g (9 oz) vermicelli
30 g (¹/₄ cup) plain (all-purpose) flour
375 ml (1¹/₄ cups) milk
155 g (1¹/₄ cups) grated Cheddar
  cheese

1 Preheat the oven to 180°C (350°F/ Gas 4). Grease a 24 cm (9¹/₂ inch) round deep springform tin. Melt 20 g (¹/₂ oz) butter in a deep frying pan and cook the onion over medium heat for 2–3 minutes, or until soft. Add the beef mince, breaking up any lumps with the back of a spoon, and cook for 4–5 minutes, or until browned. Stir in the pasta sauce and tomato paste, reduce the heat and simmer for 20–25 minutes. Season.

2 Cook the pasta in a large saucepan of boiling water until *al dente*. Drain and rinse. Melt the remaining butter in a saucepan over low heat. Stir in the flour and cook for 1 minute, or until pale and foaming. Remove from heat and gradually stir in the milk. Return to the heat and stir constantly until the sauce boils and thickens. Reduce heat; simmer for 2 minutes.

3 Spread half the pasta in the tin, then cover with half the meat sauce. Cover with remaining pasta, pressing down with the palm of your hand. Spoon on remaining meat sauce; pour on the white sauce. Sprinkle with cheese and cook for 15 minutes. Stand for 10 minutes, then remove from the tin. Cut into wedges.

NUTRITION PER SERVE (6)
Fat 32 g; Protein 33.5 g; Carbohydrate 46.5 g; Dietary Fibre 5.5 g; Cholesterol 121 mg; 2535 kJ (605 Cal)

1

2

3

PASTA PRONTO

Preparation time: 10 minutes
Cooking time: 15 minutes
Serves 4

2 tablespoons extra virgin olive oil
4 garlic cloves, finely chopped
1 small red chilli, finely chopped
3 x 400 g (14 oz) cans crushed
   tomatoes
1 teaspoon sugar
80 ml (1/3 cup) dry white wine
3 tablespoons chopped fresh herbs
   (e.g. basil or parsley)
400 g (14 oz) vermicelli
30 g (1 oz) shaved Parmesan cheese

1 Heat the oil in a large deep frying pan and cook the garlic and chilli for 1 minute. Add the tomato, sugar, wine, herbs and 440 ml (1³/₄ cups) water. Bring to the boil and season.
2 Reduce the heat to medium and add the pasta, breaking the strands if they are too long. Cook for 10 minutes, or until the pasta is cooked, stirring often to stop the pasta from sticking. The pasta will thicken the sauce as it cooks. Season to taste and serve in bowls with shaved Parmesan.

NUTRITION PER SERVE
Fat 13.5 g; Protein 17 g; Carbohydrate 81.5 g; Dietary Fibre 9.5 g; Cholesterol 7 mg; 2225 kJ (530 Cal)

1

2

ZITI CARBONARA

Preparation time: 15 minutes
Cooking time: 15 minutes
Serves 4–6

500 g (1 lb 2 oz) ziti
1 tablespoon olive oil
200 g (7 oz) piece pancetta, cut into
    long thin strips
4 egg yolks
300 ml (10½ fl oz) cream
50 g (½ cup) grated Parmesan cheese
2 tablespoons finely chopped fresh
    flat-leaf (Italian) parsley

1 Cook the pasta in a large saucepan of boiling water until *al dente*. Drain well and return to the pan.

Meanwhile, heat the olive oil in a non-stick frying pan and cook the pancetta over high heat for 6 minutes, or until crisp and golden.
2 Beat the egg yolks, cream and Parmesan together in a bowl and season generously. Pour over the hot pasta in the saucepan and toss gently. Add the pancetta and parsley. Return the pan to very low heat and cook for 30 seconds to 1 minute, or until the sauce has thickened and coats the pasta. Don't cook over high heat or the eggs will scramble. Season with salt and pepper and serve immediately with extra Parmesan, if desired.

NUTRITION PER SERVE (6)
Fat 35.5 g; Protein 21.5 g; Carbohydrate 60 g; Dietary Fibre 4 g; Cholesterol 213.5 mg; 2700 kJ (645 Cal)

1

2

SMOKED CHICKEN LINGUINE

Preparation time: 15 minutes
Cooking time: 20 minutes
Serves 4

1 tablespoon olive oil
1 leek, thinly sliced
3 large garlic cloves, finely chopped
125 ml ($\frac{1}{2}$ cup) dry white wine
300 g (10$\frac{1}{2}$ oz) Swiss brown
    mushrooms, sliced
2 teaspoons chopped fresh thyme
300 ml (10$\frac{1}{2}$ oz) thick (double/heavy)
    cream
2 smoked chicken breast fillets,
    thinly sliced (see Note)
350 g (12 oz) fresh linguine

1 Heat the oil in a saucepan. Add the leek and cook, stirring, over low heat for 3–4 minutes, or until soft. Add the garlic and cook for another minute. Pour in the wine and simmer for 2–3 minutes, or until the liquid has reduced by half.

2 Increase the heat to medium, add the mushrooms and thyme and cook for 5 minutes, or until any excess liquid has been absorbed, then add the cream and sliced chicken. Reduce the heat and simmer for 4–5 minutes, or until the sauce has slightly thickened. Meanwhile, cook the pasta in a large saucepan of boiling water until *al dente*. Drain and divide among serving plates. Spoon on the sauce and serve.

NUTRITION PER SERVE
Fat 39.5 g; Protein 32.5 g; Carbohydrate 52.5 g; Dietary Fibre 4 g; Cholesterol 206.5 mg; 2990 kJ (715 Cal)

COOK'S FILE
Note: You can buy smoked chicken at the deli section of some supermarkets and good delicatessens.

1

2

SPAGHETTINI WITH HERBS, BABY SPINACH AND GARLIC CRUMBS

Preparation time: 15 minutes
Cooking time: 15 minutes
Serves 4

375 g (13 oz) spaghettini
125 g (4½ oz) day-old crusty Italian bread, crusts removed
100 ml (3½ fl oz) extra virgin olive oil, plus extra for drizzling
4 garlic cloves, finely chopped
400 g (14 oz) baby spinach leaves
25 g (½ cup) chopped fresh flat-leaf (Italian) parsley
4 tablespoons chopped fresh basil
1 tablespoon fresh thyme leaves
30 g (1 oz) shaved Parmesan cheese

1 Cook the pasta in a large saucepan of boiling water until *al dente*. Drain, reserving 125 ml (½ cup) of the pasta water. Return the pasta to the saucepan and keep warm.

2 To make the garlic breadcrumbs, place the crustless bread in a food processor or blender and pulse until coarse breadcrumbs form. Heat 1 tablespoon of the oil in a saucepan. Add the breadcrumbs and half the garlic and toss for 2–3 minutes, or until lightly golden. Remove, then wipe the pan clean with paper towel.

3 Heat 2 tablespoons of the oil in the same pan. Add the spinach and remaining garlic, toss together for 1 minute, then add the herbs. Cook, tossing frequently, for a further 1 minute to wilt the herbs a little and to heat through. Toss the spinach mixture through the pasta with the remaining oil and reserved pasta water. Divide among four serving bowls and scatter with the garlic crumbs. Serve hot sprinkled with Parmesan and drizzled with extra virgin olive oil.

NUTRITION PER SERVE
Fat 23.5 g; Protein 19 g; Carbohydrate 82 g; Dietary Fibre 9 g; Cholesterol 7 mg; 2590 kJ (620 Cal)

AGNOLOTTI

CONCHIGLIONE

RAVIOLI

TORTELLINI

FILLED

Like a carefully chosen present, filled pasta is as good on the inside as on the outside. A delectable filling is enclosed by a pasta wrapping perfect in its simplicity.

AGNOLOTTI: The name for filled pasta in the Piedmont region of Italy, agnolotti can be shaped into squares, crescents or circles, and usually have ruffled edges. Agnolotti was originally used to wrap up leftovers of meat and sausage in fresh pasta.

Chicken agnolotti: Pasta filled with chicken mince, often combined with cheese, spinach or another meat. Any other chicken-filled pasta can be used instead.

Ricotta agnolotti: The ricotta filling is the same as that used in ravioli and tortellini and the three shapes are interchangeable.

Veal agnolotti: Meat is the most common filling for agnolotti—predominantly veal combined with other meats. These can be substituted with other pasta shapes filled with veal, such as ravioli or tortellini. The best sauce for veal-filled pastas is a simple cream, cheese or butter-based sauce that does not compete with the flavours of the filling.

CONCHIGLIONE (large shells): Part of the conchiglie (shell) family of pasta (see page 7 for more information), conchiglione is the largest of the shells. It is usually stuffed with a filling and baked in a ceramic dish: its shape makes it a natural for stuffing as the hollow centre is excellent for holding cheese, meat or seafood and sauce. It can be substituted with other large pasta shapes including large rigatoni (page 7) or lumaconi, the giant pasta snails (not shown).

RAVIOLI: The most recognised filled pasta outside Italy, ravioli are little stuffed square pasta pillows.

Chicken ravioli: Chicken ravioli are usually made out of a mixture of chicken, cheese and either a meat such as pork or prosciutto, or with the addition of spinach. You can use another chicken-filled pasta instead.

Ricotta ravioli: The simple ricotta filling makes this a very versatile pasta suitable for many different flavoured sauces. The filling will sometimes be wrapped in plain pasta and sometimes with a flavoured pasta, such as spinach. Any ricotta-filled pasta will work just as well.

Seafood ravioli: A variety of seafood can be used to fill ravioli, including fish, smoked salmon and crustaceans. Small seafood such as prawns and scallops are ideal fillings as their texture and flavour are well matched to being encased in pasta, cooked quickly and dressed with oil or butter and herbs or creamy sauces. Usually only available at pasta shops or delicatessens.

Spinach ravioli: Ravioli with ricotta and spinach is known as 'di magro' in Italian, meaning lean. To make this favourite filling, spinach is combined with ricotta, Parmesan and nutmeg. It can be replaced with spinach tortellini or agnolotti.

Veal ravioli: A filling of veal mixed with minced pork, Parmesan and nutmeg is excellent served with a herb-flavoured butter. Replace with another veal-filled pasta.

TORTELLINI: Originating in Bologna, these small pasta rings are said to be named after Venus' navel. There are several popular fillings.

Cheese tortellini: Cheese is by far the most widely available and simplest filling for tortellini. The usual cheese filling is made up of a mixture of ricotta with a small amount of Parmesan, but a range of other cheeses can be used instead, including provolone, Gruyère, goat's cheese and fontina. Cheese tortellini can be replaced with cheese ravioli or agnolotti.

Ham and cheese tortellini: Using the classic combination of ham and cheese, this is a perennial favourite. The mixture of cooked ham, Parmesan, nutmeg and fresh herbs is well suited to a herb-flavoured butter sauce. Mortadella or Italian sausage are sometimes used as a variation to the ham. Substitute other pastas with the same filling.

Veal tortellini: The filling is usually made up of predominantly veal mixed with other meats (for example, pork, mortadella and prosciutto). Sometimes Parmesan and spices, such as nutmeg, are added to the mixture. Traditionally these little pasta crescents are served in Bologna's speciality 'tortellini in brodo', which is in consommé, or with melted butter and cheese. Other veal-filled pastas can be used instead.

VEAL AGNOLOTTI WITH ALFREDO SAUCE

Preparation time: 10 minutes
Cooking time: 10 minutes
Serves 4–6

625 g (1 lb 6 oz) veal agnolotti
90 g (3¼ oz) butter
150 g (1½ cups) grated Parmesan
   cheese
300 ml (10½ fl oz) cream
2 tablespoons chopped fresh
   marjoram

1 Cook the pasta in a large saucepan of boiling water until *al dente*. Drain and return to the pan.
2 Just before the pasta is cooked, melt the butter in a saucepan over low heat. Add the Parmesan and cream and bring to the boil. Reduce the heat and simmer, stirring constantly, for 2 minutes, or until the sauce has thickened slightly. Stir in the marjoram and season with salt and ground black pepper. Toss the sauce through the pasta until well coated and serve immediately.

NUTRITION PER SERVE (6)
Fat 48.5 g; Protein 21.5 g; Carbohydrate 39.5 g; Dietary Fibre 3.5 g; Cholesterol 156.5 mg; 2835 kJ (680 Cal)

COOK'S FILE
Variation: Marjoram can be replaced with any other fresh herb you prefer—for example, try parsley, thyme, chervil or dill.

1

2

CHEESE TORTELLINI WITH CAPSICUM AND ALMOND SAUCE

Preparation time: 15 minutes
Cooking time: 15 minutes
Serves 4

1 red capsicum (pepper)
1 yellow capsicum (pepper)
60 g (2/3 cup) flaked almonds
8 spring onions (scallions)
2 garlic cloves, crushed
500 g (1 lb 2 oz) cheese tortellini
170 ml (2/3 cup) olive oil
30 g (1/3 cup) finely grated pecorino cheese

1 Cut the capsicums into large pieces, removing the seeds and membrane. Place, skin-side-up, under a hot grill (broiler) until the skin blackens and blisters. Cool in a plastic bag, then peel away the skin. Spread the almonds on a grill tray and grill for 1–2 minutes, or until lightly toasted.

2 Roughly chop the white part of the spring onions and slice the green tops, reserving for garnish. Put the capsicum, almonds, garlic and white part of the spring onion in a food processor and pulse until chopped.

3 Cook the pasta in a large saucepan of boiling water until *al dente*. Drain and return to the pan. Toss the capsicum mixture through the pasta, then add the oil and cheese. Season to taste. Serve garnished with the reserved green spring onion.

NUTRITION PER SERVE
Fat 63.5 g; Protein 23.5 g; Carbohydrate 35.5 g; Dietary Fibre 6.5 g; Cholesterol 49 mg; 3355 kJ (800 Cal)

RICOTTA AGNOLOTTI WITH SALMON, CAPERS AND BROWN BUTTER

Preparation time: 10 minutes
Cooking time: 15 minutes
Serves 4

125 ml (1/2 cup) olive oil
100 g (3 1/2 oz) capers, drained and patted dry
500 g (1 lb 2 oz) salmon fillets, skin removed
625 g (1 lb 6 oz) ricotta agnolotti
150 g (5 1/2 oz) butter
1 1/2 teaspoons finely grated lemon zest
2 tablespoons lemon juice
3 tablespoons roughly chopped fresh flat-leaf (Italian) parsley

1 Heat half the oil in a small frying pan and cook the capers over high heat for 3–4 minutes, or until golden and crispy. Remove from the oil, drain on paper towel and set aside.
2 Season the salmon fillets on both sides with salt and pepper. Heat the remaining oil in a non-stick frying pan and cook the salmon for 2–3 minutes each side, or until just cooked through but still pink in the centre. Remove from the pan and keep warm. Gently break the salmon into flakes with your fingers, being careful to remove any bones.
3 Cook the pasta in a large saucepan of boiling water until *al dente*. Drain, return to the pan and keep warm. Heat the butter in a frying pan over low heat for 5 minutes, or until golden. Quickly add the lemon zest, lemon juice and parsley. Divide the pasta among serving dishes, top with the flaked salmon and pour on the brown butter. Scatter with the capers and serve immediately.

NUTRITION PER SERVE
Fat 68 g; Protein 35.5 g; Carbohydrate 43.5 g; Dietary Fibre 5 g; Cholesterol 181 mg; 3865 kJ (925 Cal)

VEAL TORTELLINI WITH BAKED PUMPKIN AND BASIL BUTTER

Preparation time: 15 minutes
Cooking time: 30 minutes
Serves 4

1 kg (2 lb 4 oz) jap pumpkin, cut into
    2 cm (^{3}/$_4$ inch) cubes
600 g (1 lb 5 oz) veal tortellini with
    cracked pepper
100 g (3^1/$_2$ oz) butter
3 garlic cloves, crushed
80 g (^{1}/$_2$ cup) pine nuts
45 g (^{3}/$_4$ cup) firmly packed shredded
    fresh basil
200 g (7 oz) feta cheese, crumbled

1 Preheat the oven to 220°C (425°F/ Gas 7). Line a baking tray with baking paper. Place the pumpkin on the tray and season well. Bake for 30 minutes, or until tender.

2 Meanwhile, cook the pasta in a large saucepan of boiling water until *al dente*. Drain and return to the pan. Heat the butter over medium heat in a small frying pan until foaming. Add the garlic and pine nuts and cook for 3–5 minutes, or until the nuts are starting to turn golden. Remove from the heat and add the basil. Toss the basil butter, pumpkin and feta through the cooked pasta and serve immediately.

NUTRITION PER SERVE
Fat 57 g; Protein 33.5 g; Carbohydrate 72 g; Dietary Fibre 10 g; Cholesterol 136.5 mg; 3900 kJ (930 Cal)

TORTELLINI WITH SPECK, ASPARAGUS AND FRESH TOMATO

Preparation time: 15 minutes
Cooking time: 15 minutes
Serves 4–6

200 g (7 oz) piece speck (skin removed), roughly chopped
4 tomatoes
310 g (10¾ oz) asparagus, cut into 3 cm (1¼ inch) lengths
500 g (1 lb 2 oz) cheese tortellini
1 tablespoon olive oil
1 red onion, thinly sliced
1 tablespoon tomato paste (purée)
125 ml (½ cup) chicken stock
2 teaspoons fresh thyme leaves

1 Place the speck in a food processor and pulse until chopped. Score a cross in the base of each tomato, place in a heatproof bowl and cover with boiling water. Leave for 1 minute, then plunge into cold water and peel the skin away from the cross. Roughly chop.

2 Cook the asparagus in a large saucepan of boiling water for 2 minutes, or until just tender, then remove and refresh in cold water. Drain. Add the pasta to the same boiling water and cook until *al dente*. Drain and keep warm.

3 Meanwhile, heat the oil in a saucepan, add the speck and onion and cook, stirring, over medium heat for 2–3 minutes, or until the onion is soft. Add the tomato, tomato paste, stock and thyme and season to taste with salt and ground black pepper. Cook, stirring, for 5 minutes. Add the pasta and asparagus to the tomato mixture and stir over low heat until warmed through. Divide among warmed bowls and serve.

NUTRITION PER SERVE (6)
Fat 18 g; Protein 21.5 g; Carbohydrate 25 g; Dietary Fibre 4.5 g; Cholesterol 52.5 mg; 1455 kJ (345 Cal)

1

2

3

VEAL TORTELLINI WITH CREAMY MUSHROOM SAUCE

Preparation time: 15 minutes
Cooking time: 20 minutes
Serves 4

500 g (1 lb 2 oz) veal tortellini
60 ml (1/4 cup) olive oil
600 g (1 lb 5 oz) Swiss brown
   mushrooms, thinly sliced
2 garlic cloves, crushed
125 ml (1/2 cup) dry white wine
300 ml (10 1/2 fl oz) thick
   (double/heavy) cream
pinch ground nutmeg
3 tablespoons finely chopped fresh
   flat-leaf (Italian) parsley
30 g (1 oz) grated Parmesan cheese

1 Cook the pasta in a large saucepan of boiling water until *al dente*. Drain. Meanwhile, heat the oil in a frying pan over medium heat. Add the mushrooms and cook, stirring occasionally, for 5 minutes, or until softened. Add the garlic and cook for 1 minute, then stir in the wine and cook for 5 minutes, or until the liquid has reduced by half.
2 Add the cream, nutmeg and parsley, stir to combine and cook for 3–5 minutes, or until it thickens slightly. Season. Divide the tortellini among four bowls and spoon on the sauce and sprinkle with Parmesan.

NUTRITION PER SERVE
Fat 52.5 g; Protein 23.5 g; Carbohydrate 50 g;
Dietary Fibre 8.5 g; Cholesterol 125 mg;
3275 kJ (785 Cal)

1

2

SPINACH RAVIOLI WITH SEMI-DRIED TOMATOES AND PINE NUT SALSA

Preparation time: 15 minutes
Cooking time: 10 minutes
Serves 4

625 g (1 lb 6 oz) spinach ravioli
3¹/₂ tablespoons olive oil
50 g (¹/₃ cup) pine nuts
150 g (5¹/₂ oz) semi-dried (sun-blushed) tomatoes, thinly sliced

270 g (9¹/₂ oz) jar roasted capsicums (peppers), drained and thinly sliced
2 tablespoons finely chopped fresh flat-leaf (Italian) parsley
2 tablespoons finely chopped fresh mint
1¹/₂ tablespoons balsamic vinegar
30 g (1 oz) shaved Parmesan cheese

1 Cook the pasta in a large saucepan of boiling water until *al dente*. Drain. Heat ¹/₂ teaspoon of the oil in a frying pan and gently cook the pine nuts until light gold. Remove from the pan and roughly chop.

2 Add the remaining oil to the pan and add the tomato, capsicum, parsley, mint and vinegar and stir until combined and warmed through. Remove from the heat and season to taste. Stir in the pine nuts. Divide the pasta among four serving plates, spoon on the sauce and top with the Parmesan. Serve immediately.

NUTRITION PER SERVE
Fat 29.5 g; Protein 19.5 g; Carbohydrate 46.5 g; Dietary Fibre 8.5 g; Cholesterol 31.5 mg; 2225 kJ (530 Cal)

RAVIOLI WITH PRAWNS AND KAFFIR LIME SAUCE

Preparation time: 15 minutes
Cooking time: 20 minutes
Serves 4

50 g (1³⁄₄ oz) butter
4 garlic cloves, crushed
750 g (1 lb 10 oz) medium raw prawns (shrimp), peeled and deveined
1¹⁄₂ tablespoons plain (all-purpose) flour
375 ml (1¹⁄₂ cups) fish stock
500 ml (2 cups) cream
5 makrut (kaffir) lime leaves, shredded
625 g (1 lb 6 oz) seafood ravioli (see Note)
3 teaspoons fish sauce

1 Melt the butter in a deep large frying pan and cook the garlic over medium heat for 1 minute. Add the prawns and cook for 3–4 minutes, or until they turn pink and are cooked through. Remove from the pan, leaving any juices in the pan. Add the flour and stir for 1 minute, or until light golden. Gradually stir in the stock, then add the cream and kaffir lime leaves. Reduce the heat and simmer for 10 minutes, or until slightly thickened.

2 Meanwhile, cook the pasta in a large saucepan of boiling water until *al dente*. Drain. Stir the fish sauce through the cream sauce, add the prawns and stir until warmed through. Divide the pasta among four warm serving plates and spoon on the prawns and sauce. Season to taste with salt and ground black pepper and serve immediately.

NUTRITION PER SERVE
Fat 75.5 g; Protein 42 g; Carbohydrate 62.5 g; Dietary Fibre 5.5 g; Cholesterol 428.5 mg; 4575 kJ (1095 Cal)

COOK'S FILE
Note: Seafood ravioli is available from speciality pasta shops, but if it is unavailable, you can use ricotta ravioli instead—the flavours work well.

SALMON AND RICOTTA-STUFFED CONCHIGLIONE

Preparation time: 15 minutes
Cooking time: 40 minutes
Serves 4

200 g (7 oz) (about 32) conchiglione
(large shells)
425 g (15 oz) can good-quality red
salmon, drained, bones removed,
flaked
500 g (1 lb 2 oz) fresh ricotta cheese
1 tablespoon chopped fresh flat-leaf
(Italian) parsley
3 tablespoons chopped fresh chives
1½ celery sticks, finely chopped
90 g (¾ cup) grated Cheddar cheese
185 ml (¾ cup) cream
25 g (¼ cup) grated Parmesan
cheese

1 Preheat the oven to 180°C
(350°F/Gas 4). Cook the pasta in a
large saucepan of boiling water for
4–5 minutes. Drain.
2 Combine the salmon, ricotta,
parsley, chives, celery and Cheddar
in a bowl and season to taste with
salt and ground black pepper.
3 Place 2 teaspoons of filling in each
shell and transfer the filled shells
to a 3 litre (12 cup) 26 x 36 x 7 cm
(10½ x 14½ x 2¾ inch) ceramic
baking dish. Once they are all in the
dish, pour on the cream and sprinkle
with Parmesan. Cover with foil and
bake for 20 minutes, then remove
the foil and return to the oven for
15 minutes, or until golden brown.
Serve in pasta bowls with the sauce
spooned over the shells.

NUTRITION PER SERVE
Fat 35.5 g; Protein 31 g; Carbohydrate 37.5 g;
Dietary Fibre 3 g; Cholesterol 135 mg;
2470 kJ (590 Cal)

1

2

3

SPINACH RAVIOLI WITH ROASTED TOMATOES AND GOAT'S CHEESE

Preparation time: 15 minutes
Cooking time: 1 hour
Serves 4

4 Roma (plum) tomatoes
6 garlic cloves, unpeeled and bruised
80 ml (1/3 cup) extra virgin olive oil
2 1/2 teaspoons caster (superfine) sugar
500 g (1 lb 2 oz) spinach ravioli
2 tablespoons red wine vinegar
90 g (3 1/4 oz) pitted Kalamata olives
100 g (3 1/2 oz) baby spinach leaves
100 g (3 1/2 oz) goat's cheese, crumbled

1 Preheat the oven to 190°C (375°F/Gas 5). Cut the tomatoes into quarters, then cut each quarter in half. Place the tomatoes and garlic on a large greased baking tray. Drizzle with 1 tablespoon of the olive oil, sprinkle with 1 teaspoon of the sugar and season. Roast for 1 hour, or until softened and caramelized. Remove and keep warm.

2 Just before the tomatoes are ready, cook the pasta in a large saucepan of boiling water until *al dente*. Drain and place in a large bowl. Remove the skins from the garlic.

3 To make the dressing, combine the remaining extra virgin olive oil with the red wine vinegar, roasted garlic and the remaining sugar in a screw-top jar and shake until well combined. Pour over the pasta and toss gently. Add the olives, baby spinach leaves, goat's cheese and roasted tomato and toss together. Serve immediately.

NUTRITION PER SERVE
Fat 25 g; Protein 14.5 g; Carbohydrate 39.5 g; Dietary Fibre 6 g; Cholesterol 29.5 mg; 1850 kJ (440 Cal)

1

2

3

CHICKEN RAVIOLI WITH PESTO

Preparation time: 10 minutes
Cooking time: 10 minutes
Serves 4

625 g (1 lb 6 oz) chicken ravioli
50 g (1 cup) firmly packed fresh basil
2 garlic cloves
40 g (1/4 cup) pine nuts, toasted
125 ml (1/2 cup) extra virgin olive oil
50 g (1/2 cup) grated Parmesan cheese
50 g (1 3/4 oz) pecorino cheese, grated
15 g (1/4 cup) firmly packed fresh
   basil, extra, torn
30 g (1 oz) shaved Parmesan cheese,
   to serve

1 Cook the pasta in a large saucepan of boiling water until *al dente*. Meanwhile, blend the basil, garlic, pine nuts and olive oil in a food processor or blender until smooth. Stir in the grated Parmesan and pecorino and season to taste with salt and pepper.
2 Drain the pasta, reserving 1 tablespoon of the cooking water to add to the pesto. Carefully toss the ravioli in the pesto and reserved water and finish with a drizzle of extra virgin olive oil, a little torn basil and some Parmesan shavings.

NUTRITION PER SERVE
Fat 54 g; Protein 30 g; Carbohydrate 57.5 g; Dietary Fibre 6.5 g; Cholesterol 83 mg; 3490 kJ (835 Cal)

PASTA WITH CREAMY SEMI-DRIED TOMATO SAUCE AND BACON

Preparation time: 10 minutes
Cooking time: 20 minutes
Serves 4

4 rashers bacon
625 g (1 lb 6 oz) veal or chicken
    agnolotti
1 tablespoon olive oil
2 garlic cloves, finely chopped
110 g (²/3 cup) thinly sliced semi-
    dried (sun-blushed) tomatoes
1 tablespoon chopped fresh thyme
375 ml (1¹/2 cups) cream
1 teaspoon finely grated lemon zest
35 g (¹/3 cup) finely grated Parmesan
    cheese

1 Grill (broil) the bacon for 5 minutes each side, or until crisp and golden. Remove, drain well on paper towel, then break into pieces.
2 Cook the pasta in a large saucepan of boiling water until *al dente*. Drain and keep warm. Heat the oil in a frying pan and cook the garlic over medium heat for 1 minute, or until just golden. Add the tomato and thyme and cook for 1 minute more.
3 Add the cream, bring to the boil, then reduce the heat and simmer for 6–8 minutes, or until the cream has thickened and reduced by one third. Season with salt and pepper, add the lemon zest, and 2 tablespoons of the Parmesan. Divide the pasta among four serving bowls and pour on the sauce. Sprinkle with the remaining Parmesan and the bacon pieces. Serve immediately.

NUTRITION PER SERVE
Fat 60.5 g; Protein 32 g; Carbohydrate 64.5 g; Dietary Fibre 7.5 g; Cholesterol 212 mg; 3895 kJ (930 Cal)

VEAL RAVIOLI WITH HERB BUTTER

Preparation time: 10 minutes
Cooking time: 10 minutes
Serves 4

500 g (1 lb 2 oz) good-quality veal ravioli
100 g (3½ oz) butter, softened
3 garlic cloves, crushed
2 tablespoons finely chopped fresh flat-leaf (Italian) parsley
2 teaspoons finely chopped fresh sage
2 teaspoons chopped fresh thyme
60 ml (¼ cup) white wine
1 large vine-ripened tomato, finely diced

1 Cook the pasta in a large saucepan of boiling water until *al dente*. Drain, return to the pan and keep warm.
2 Meanwhile, melt the butter in a large frying pan over medium heat. Add the garlic and herbs and cook, stirring, for 1 minute. Add the wine and cook for another minute. Pour over the pasta, add the tomato and toss over medium heat until warmed through. Divide among four serving plates and serve.

NUTRITION PER SERVE
Fat 29 g; Protein 14 g; Carbohydrate 46.5 g; Dietary Fibre 5.5 g; Cholesterol 96 mg; 2140 kJ (510 Cal)

1

2

RICOTTA AND PROSCIUTTO-FILLED CONCHIGLIONE

Preparation time: 15 minutes
Cooking time: 40 minutes
Serves 4–6

24 conchiglione (large shells)
200 g (7 oz) prosciutto, roughly
    chopped
2 tablespoons chopped fresh
    chives
60 g (1 cup) chopped fresh basil
80 g (2³/4 oz) butter
500 g (1 lb 2 oz) fresh ricotta cheese

150 g (1 cup) chopped sun-dried
    (sun-blushed) capsicum (pepper)
100 g (1 cup) grated Parmesan
    cheese
750 g (3 cups) bottled tomato pasta
    sauce

1 Preheat the oven to 180°C (350°F/ Gas 4). Cook the pasta in a large saucepan of boiling water until *al dente*. Drain. Place the prosciutto, chives and basil in a food processor or blender and pulse until chopped.
2 Melt the butter in a large frying pan over medium heat. Add the prosciutto mixture and cook for 5 minutes, or until the prosciutto is golden and crisp. Transfer the mixture to a bowl, add the ricotta, capsicum and 25 g (¹/4 cup) of the Parmesan. Stir well. Season to taste.
3 Pour the pasta sauce into a 3 litre (12 cup) ovenproof ceramic baking dish. Spoon the ricotta mixture into the pasta shells and place into the baking dish. Sprinkle the remaining Parmesan over the shells and bake for 25–30 minutes, or until the tops of the shells turn golden. Spoon the sauce over the shells and serve.

NUTRITION PER SERVE (6)
Fat 28 g; Protein 27 g; Carbohydrate 31.5 g;
Dietary Fibre 4.5 g; Cholesterol 107 mg;
2040 kJ (485 Cal)

1

2

3

RAVIOLI WITH ROASTED RED CAPSICUM SAUCE

Preparation time: 15 minutes
Cooking time: 15 minutes
Serves 4

6 red capsicums (peppers)
6 slices prosciutto
625 g (1 lb 6 oz) chicken or ricotta
    ravioli
2 tablespoons olive oil
3 garlic cloves, crushed
2 leeks, thinly sliced
1 tablespoon chopped fresh oregano
2 teaspoons soft brown sugar
250 ml (1 cup) hot chicken stock

1 Cut the capsicums into large pieces, removing the seeds and membrane. Place, skin-side-up, under a hot grill (broiler) until the skin blackens and blisters. Cool in a plastic bag, then peel away the skin. Place the prosciutto under the grill and cook for 1 minute each side, or until crisp. Break into pieces and set aside.

2 Cook the pasta in a large saucepan of boiling water until *al dente*. Meanwhile, heat the oil in a frying pan and cook the garlic and leek over medium heat for 3–4 minutes, or until softened. Add the oregano and sugar and stir for 1 minute.

3 Place the capsicum and leek mixture in a food processor or blender, season with salt and pepper and process until combined. Add the chicken stock and process until smooth. Drain the pasta and return to the saucepan. Gently toss the sauce through the ravioli over low heat until warmed through. Divide among four serving bowls and sprinkle with prosciutto.

NUTRITION PER SERVE
Fat 20 g; Protein 25 g; Carbohydrate 59 g;
Dietary Fibre 8.5 g; Cholesterol 56.5 mg;
2150 kJ (515 Cal)

HAM TORTELLINI WITH NUTTY HERB SAUCE

Preparation time: 15 minutes
Cooking time: 10 minutes
Serves 4–6

500 g (1 lb 2 oz) ham and cheese
    tortellini
60 g (2¼ oz) butter
100 g (1 cup) walnuts, chopped
100 g (²/3 cup) pine nuts
2 tablespoons finely chopped fresh
    flat-leaf (Italian) parsley
2 teaspoons chopped fresh thyme
60 g (¼ cup) fresh ricotta cheese

60 ml (¼ cup) thick (double/heavy)
    cream

1 Cook the pasta in a large saucepan of boiling water until *al dente*. Drain and return to the pan. Heat the butter in a frying pan over medium heat until foaming. Add the nuts and stir for 5 minutes, or until golden brown. Add the herbs and season.
2 Beat the ricotta and cream together. Add the nutty sauce to the pasta and toss. Serve topped with ricotta cream.

NUTRITION PER SERVE (6)
Fat 47 g; Protein 21.5 g; Carbohydrate 23 g; Dietary Fibre 3.5 g; Cholesterol 84.5 mg; 2495 kJ (595 Cal)

LASAGNE

LASAGNETTE

PAPPARDELLE

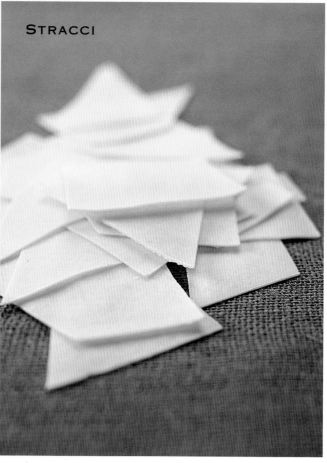

STRACCI

FLAT

Not content to be the poor relation, flat pasta makes its biggest impact by layering sheets of pasta with a delicious filling. Lasagne is always a favourite, but it is only one of many mouth-watering options using flat pasta.

LASAGNE: The name lasagne refers to the pasta sheet, not the meal of the same name.

Dried lasagne: Dried lasagne sheets are readily available from the supermarket and are best cooked as their packet instructions indicate. These large sheets of dried pasta are used for making baked, layered pasta dishes and are increasingly being used for free-form pasta stacks.

Fresh lasagne: The starting point for all fresh pasta, lasagne sheets are traditionally used for layered, baked pasta dishes. Fresh sheets are available from some supermarkets and delicatessens. Originating from Emilia–Romana (an area in northern Italy), the classic baked dish *al forno* is still the most popularly known lasagne dish with layers of lasagne sheets, a rich meat ragout and béchamel sauce with a topping of Parmesan. Other regions of Italy have their own variations of lasagne, featuring seafood, vegetables, cured meats and sausages. Lasagne sheets can also be used to make home-made ravioli and free-form lasagne, where the cooked sheets are layered with a filling just before being served. There is no satisfactory substitute for lasagne.

LASAGNETTE: Also called mafalde or mafaldini, these wide, long fluted lengths of pasta have slightly crimped edges ideal for catching their accompanying sauce. Lasagnette is best matched with rich meat, vegetable, cream or cheese sauces. It is usually available dried, not fresh. If you can't find it, use another dried pasta of a similar length and width, such as pappardelle.

PAPPARDELLE: This pasta derives its name from the verb *pappare*, meaning 'to gobble up' in Italian.

Dried pappardelle: These dried, very wide pasta ribbons are different to most other dried pastas as their dough is enriched with eggs, which is quite unusual for a dried pasta. Their width and length are best matched with strong sauces that will cover their entire surface area. You can replace dried pappardelle with dried tagliatelle (page 47) or lasagnette, but unless you are using an egg pasta, they will not have quite the same flavour.

Fresh pappardelle: Fresh pappardelle is a wide ribbon-shaped egg noodle pasta, 20–30 cm (8–12 inch) long and 3–5 cm (1¹/4–2 inch) wide. Shorter and wider than tagliatelle, pappardelle is the traditional companion to rich game sauces such as hare. It suits sauces made with other gamey meats like rabbit, strong vegetables like fennel or raddichio and creamy sauces. If necessary, you can replace fresh pappardelle with fresh fettucine, tagliatelle (page 47) or lasagnette.

STRACCI: Made from fresh pasta sheets, stracci, meaning 'stretched' in Italian, is one of the easiest pasta shapes to make. Large pasta sheets are simply sliced into reasonably large and varied shapes by cutting different lengths along a range of angles. Stracci can be substituted quite easily by breaking dried lasagne sheets into ragged pieces about 7 x 12 cm (2³/4 x 5 inch). Any sauce that goes with stracci will also go well with fresh or dried fettucine or tagliatelle (page 47). Stracci is most often available dried.

SMOKED SALMON STRACCI IN CHAMPAGNE SAUCE

Preparation time: 15 minutes
Cooking time: 10 minutes
Serves 4

375 g (13 oz) fresh stracci
1 tablespoon olive oil
2 large garlic cloves,
    crushed
125 ml (1/2 cup) Champagne
250 ml (1 cup) thick (double/heavy)
    cream
200 g (7 oz) smoked salmon, cut into
    thin strips
2 tablespoons small capers in brine,
    rinsed and patted dry
2 tablespoons chopped fresh chives
2 tablespoons chopped fresh dill

1 Cook the pasta in a large saucepan of boiling water until *al dente*. Drain and return to the pan. Meanwhile, heat the oil in a large frying pan and cook the garlic over medium heat for 30 seconds. Pour in the Champagne and cook for 2–3 minutes, or until reduced slightly. Add the cream and cook for 3–4 minutes, or until reduced and thickened.

2 Add the sauce and remaining ingredients to the hot pasta and toss gently. Season to taste with salt and ground black pepper and serve immediately.

NUTRITION PER SERVE
Fat 32.5 g; Protein 23.5 g; Carbohydrate 54.5 g; Dietary Fibre 1.5 g; Cholesterol 164.5 mg; 2600 kJ (620 Cal)

PAPPARDELLE WITH BUG TAIL AND SAFFRON CREAM SAUCE

Preparation time: 10 minutes
Cooking time: 20 minutes
Serves 4–6

400 g (14 oz) pappardelle
60 g (2¼ oz) butter
4 large garlic cloves, crushed
250 g (9 oz) Swiss brown
  mushrooms, sliced
500 g (1 lb 2 oz) fresh or frozen raw
  bug meat or lobster tail meat

125 ml (½ cup) white wine
½ teaspoon saffron threads
700 ml (24 fl oz) thick (double/heavy)
  cream
2 egg yolks

1 Cook the pasta in a large saucepan of boiling water until *al dente*. Meanwhile, melt the butter in a large deep frying pan, add the garlic and mushrooms and cook over medium heat for 2–3 minutes, or until soft. Add the bug meat and cook for 4–5 minutes, or until just cooked through. Remove from the pan.
2 Add the wine and saffron to the pan, scraping the bottom to remove any sediment. Bring to the boil and cook for 2–3 minutes, or until reduced. Add the cream, reduce the heat and simmer for 5 minutes. Whisk through the egg yolks until thickened. Return the bug meat mixture to the pan and stir until warmed through. Drain the pasta and divide among serving dishes. Spoon on the bug meat sauce and season to taste. Serve immediately.

NUTRITION PER SERVE (6)
Fat 54.5 g; Protein 28.5 g; Carbohydrate 51.5 g; Dietary Fibre 3 g; Cholesterol 308.5 mg; 3430 kJ (820 Cal)

BLUE CHEESE AND WALNUT LASAGNETTE

Preparation time: 10 minutes
Cooking time: 15 minutes
Serves 4

375 g (13 oz) lasagnette
100 g (1 cup) walnuts
40 g (1½ oz) butter
3 French shallots, finely chopped
1 tablespoon brandy or cognac
250 ml (1 cup) crème fraîche
200 g (7 oz) gorgonzola cheese, crumbled
75 g (2½ oz) baby spinach leaves

1 Preheat the oven to 200°C (400°F/Gas 6). Cook the pasta in a large saucepan of boiling water until *al dente*. Drain, return to the pan and keep warm. Meanwhile, place the walnuts on a baking tray and roast for 5 minutes, or until golden and toasted. Cool, then roughly chop.

2 Heat the butter in a large saucepan, add the shallots and cook over medium heat for 1–2 minutes, or until soft, taking care not to brown. Add the brandy and simmer for 1 minute, then stir in the crème fraîche and gorgonzola. Cook for 3–4 minutes, or until the cheese has melted and the sauce has thickened. Stir in the spinach and toasted walnuts, reserving 1 tablespoon for garnish. Heat gently until the spinach has just wilted. Season with salt and ground black pepper. Gently mix the sauce through the pasta. Divide among serving plates and sprinkle with the reserved walnuts.

NUTRITION PER SERVE
Fat 63.5 g; Protein 31.5 g; Carbohydrate 68.5 g; Dietary Fibre 4.5 g; Cholesterol 152 mg; 4095 kJ (980 Cal)

COOK'S FILE
Note: The gorgonzola needs to be young as this gives a sweeter, milder flavour.

PAPPARDELLE WITH SALAMI, LEEK AND PROVOLONE CHEESE

Preparation time: 15 minutes
Cooking time: 15 minutes
Serves 4

375 g (13 oz) pappardelle
2 tablespoons olive oil
2 leeks, thinly sliced (including
    some of the green section)
2 tablespoons white wine
2 x 400 g (14 oz) cans diced tomatoes
150 g (5¹/₂ oz) sliced mild salami,
    cut into strips
7 g (¹/₄ cup) fresh basil leaves, torn
125 g (4¹/₂ oz) provolone cheese, cut
    into 3 cm (1¹/₄ inch) wide strips
30 g (1 oz) grated Parmesan cheese

1 Cook the pasta in a large saucepan of boiling water until *al dente*, then drain and return to the pan. Meanwhile, heat the olive oil in a large deep frying pan, add the leek and cook over low heat for 4 minutes, or until soft but not browned. Increase the heat to medium, add the wine and stir until almost evaporated.

2 Add the tomato and salami, season with salt and ground black pepper and simmer for 5 minutes, or until reduced slightly. Toss the tomato sauce mixture, basil and provolone lightly through the pasta. Sprinkle with Parmesan and serve.

NUTRITION PER SERVE
Fat 37 g; Protein 34 g; Carbohydrate 74.5 g;
Dietary Fibre 6 g; Cholesterol 94 mg;
3250 kJ (775 Cal)

1

2

BOCCONCINI, PROSCIUTTO AND SPINACH LASAGNE

Preparation time: 15 minutes +
    10 minutes standing
Cooking time: 25 minutes
Serves 4–6

600 g (1 lb 5 oz) bottled tomato
    pasta sauce
250 g (9 oz) fresh lasagne sheets
400 g (14 oz) bocconcini, thinly
    sliced
500 g (1 lb 2 oz) English spinach,
    trimmed
125 ml (1/2 cup) cream
10 thin slices prosciutto, chopped

150 g (1 cup) grated mozzarella
    cheese
50 g (1/2 cup) finely grated Parmesan
    cheese

1 Preheat the oven to 180°C
(350°F/Gas 4). Lightly grease a 3 litre
(12 cup) shallow 22 cm x 30 cm
(9 x 12 inch) ovenproof dish. Spread
half of the tomato pasta sauce over
the base of the dish. Cover the layer
of pasta sauce with a third of the
lasagne sheets. Top with half of the
bocconcini and half of the spinach.
Drizzle on half of the cream and
sprinkle with half of the prosciutto.
Season with some salt and ground
black pepper. Repeat to give two
layers, starting with half of the

remaining lasagne sheets.
2 Lay the final layer of lasagne
over the top and spread with the
remaining pasta sauce. Sprinkle
with the combined mozzarella and
Parmesan. Bake for 25 minutes,
or until cooked. Leave to stand
for 10 minutes before serving.

NUTRITION PER SERVE (6)
Fat 29.5 g; Protein 35 g; Carbohydrate 30.5 g;
Dietary Fibre 4.5 g; Cholesterol 120.5 mg;
2200 kJ (525 Cal)

1

2

ROAST PUMPKIN SAUCE ON PAPPARDELLE

Preparation time: 15 minutes
Cooking time: 35 minutes
Serves 4

1.4 kg (3 lb 2 oz) butternut pumpkin
   (squash), cut into 2 cm (³/4 inch)
   pieces
4 garlic cloves, crushed
3 teaspoons fresh thyme leaves
100 ml (3¹/2 fl oz) olive oil
500 g (1 lb 2 oz) pappardelle
2 tablespoons cream
185 ml (³/4 cup) hot chicken stock
30 g (1 oz) shaved Parmesan cheese

1 Preheat the oven to 200°C (400°F/Gas 6). Place the pumpkin, garlic, thyme and 60 ml (¹/4 cup) of the olive oil in a bowl and toss together. Season with salt, transfer to a baking tray and cook for 30 minutes, or until tender and golden. Meanwhile, cook the pasta in a large saucepan of boiling water until *al dente*. Drain and return to the pan. Toss through the remaining oil and keep warm.
2 Place the cooked pumpkin and the cream in a food processor or blender and process until smooth. Add the hot stock and process until smooth and combined. Season with salt and ground black pepper and gently toss through the warm pasta. Divide among four serving plates, sprinkle with Parmesan and extra thyme leaves, if desired, and serve immediately.

NUTRITION PER SERVE
Fat 29.5 g; Protein 26 g; Carbohydrate 109.5 g; Dietary Fibre 7.5 g; Cholesterol 43 mg; 3400 kJ (810 Cal)

COOK'S FILE
Note: The sauce becomes gluggy on standing, so serve it as soon as possible.

FREE-FORM WILD MUSHROOM LASAGNE

Preparation time: 10 minutes +
    15 minutes soaking
Cooking time: 15 minutes
Serves 4

10 g (¼ oz) dried porcini mushrooms
350 g (12 oz) mixed wild mushrooms
    (shiitake, oyster, Swiss brown)
30 g (1 oz) butter
1 small onion, halved and thinly
    sliced
1 tablespoon chopped fresh thyme
3 egg yolks
125 ml (½ cup) thick (double/heavy)
    cream
100 g (1 cup) grated Parmesan cheese
8 fresh lasagne sheets
    (10 x 25 cm/4 x 10 inch)

1   Soak the porcini in 60 ml (¼ cup) boiling water for 15 minutes. Strain through a sieve, reserving the liquid. Cut the larger mushrooms in half. Heat the butter in a frying pan and cook the onion for 1–2 minutes, or until just soft. Add the thyme, mushrooms and porcini and cook for 1–2 minutes, or until softened. Add the reserved mushroom liquid and cook for 1–2 minutes, or until the liquid has evaporated. Set aside.

2   Beat the egg yolks, cream and half the Parmesan in a large bowl. Cook the lasagne sheets in a saucepan of boiling water for 2–3 minutes, stirring gently. Drain well and toss gently in the egg mixture while hot. Reheat the mushrooms. To serve, place a sheet of folded lasagne on a plate, top with some mushrooms, then another sheet of folded lasagne. Drizzle with any remaining egg mixture and sprinkle with the remaining Parmesan.

NUTRITION PER SERVE
Fat 30 g; Protein 20 g; Carbohydrate 30 g;
Dietary Fibre 4.5 g; Cholesterol 213 mg;
1950 kJ (465 Cal)

CREAMY CHICKEN AND PEPPERCORN PAPPARDELLE

Preparation time: 15 minutes
Cooking time: 15 minutes
Serves 4

2 chicken breast fillets
    (420 g/15 oz in total)
30 g (1 oz) butter
1 onion, halved and thinly sliced
2 tablespoons drained green
    peppercorns, slightly crushed
125 ml (1/2 cup) white wine

300 ml (10 1/2 fl oz) cream
400 g (14 oz) fresh pappardelle
80 g (1/3 cup) sour cream (optional)
2 tablespoons chopped fresh chives

1   Cut the chicken in half so that you have four flat fillets and season with salt and pepper. Melt the butter in a frying pan, add the chicken and cook for 3 minutes each side, or until lightly browned and cooked through. Remove from the pan, cut into slices and keep warm.

2   Add the onion and peppercorns to the same pan and cook over medium heat for 3 minutes, or until the onion has softened slightly. Add the wine and cook for 1 minute, or until reduced by half. Stir in the cream and cook for 4–5 minutes, or until thickened slightly, then season. Meanwhile, cook the pasta in a large saucepan of boiling water until *al dente*, then drain. Mix together the pasta, chicken and any juices and cream sauce. Divide the pasta among serving bowls, top with a dollop of sour cream and sprinkle with chives.

NUTRITION PER SERVE
Fat 50 g; Protein 37.5 g; Carbohydrate 59.5 g; Dietary Fibre 1.5 g; Cholesterol 250 mg; 3580 kJ (855 Cal)

ALASAGNETTE WITH SPICY CHICKEN MEATBALLS

Preparation time: 10 minutes
Cooking time: 15 minutes
Serves 4

750 g (1 lb 10 oz) minced (ground) chicken
2 tablespoons chopped fresh coriander (cilantro) leaves
1½ tablespoons red curry paste
2 tablespoons oil
1 red onion, finely chopped

3 garlic cloves, crushed
875 g (3½ cups) tomato pasta sauce
2 teaspoons soft brown sugar
350 g (12 oz) lasagnette

1 Line a tray with baking paper. Combine the meat, coriander and 1 tablespoon of the curry paste. Roll heaped tablespoons of the mixture into balls and put on the tray—about 20 balls. Refrigerate until ready.
2 Heat the oil in a large deep frying pan and cook the onion and garlic over medium heat for 2–3 minutes, or until softened. Add the remaining curry paste and cook, stirring, for

1 minute, or until fragrant. Add the pasta sauce and sugar and stir well. Reduce the heat, add the meatballs and cook, turning halfway through, for 10 minutes, or until the meatballs are cooked through.
3 Meanwhile, cook the pasta in a large saucepan of boiling water until *al dente*. Drain and divide among four serving bowls. Top with the sauce and meatballs and sprinkle with fresh coriander, if desired.

NUTRITION PER SERVE
Fat 29 g; Protein 51.5 g; Carbohydrate 79 g; Dietary Fibre 8.5 g; Cholesterol 184.5 mg; 3300 kJ (790 Cal)

1

2

3

FREE-FORM PUMPKIN, SPINACH AND RICOTTA LASAGNE

Preparation time: 15 minutes
Cooking time: 15 minutes
Serves 4

60 ml (¼ cup) olive oil
1.5 kg (3 lb 5 oz) butternut pumpkin (squash), cut into 1.5 cm (⁵/₈ inch) dice
500 g (1 lb 2 oz) English spinach leaves, thoroughly washed
4 fresh lasagne sheets (12 x 20 cm/5 x 8 inch)
500 g (2 cups) fresh ricotta cheese
2 tablespoons cream
25 g (¼ cup) grated Parmesan cheese
pinch ground nutmeg

1 Heat the oil in a large non-stick frying pan over medium heat. Add the pumpkin and toss together. Cook, stirring occasionally, for 15 minutes, or until tender (don't worry if the pumpkin is slightly mashed). Season and keep warm.
2 Meanwhile, cook the spinach in a large saucepan of boiling water for 30 seconds, or until wilted. Using a slotted spoon, transfer to a bowl of cold water. Drain well and squeeze out as much excess water as possible. Finely chop the spinach. Add the lasagne sheets to the pan of boiling water and cook, stirring occasionally, until *al dente*. Drain and lay the sheets side-by-side on a clean tea towel. Cut each sheet widthways into thirds.
3 Combine the ricotta, cream, Parmesan, spinach and nutmeg in a small pan and stir over low heat for 2–3 minutes, or until warmed through. Work quickly to assemble. Place a piece of lasagne on the base of each plate. Using half the pumpkin, top each of the sheets, then cover with another piece of lasagne. Use half the ricotta mixture to spread over the lasagne sheets, then add another lasagne piece. Top with the remaining pumpkin, then remaining ricotta mixture. Season and serve immediately.

NUTRITION PER SERVE
Fat 34.5 g; Protein 27.5 g; Carbohydrate 40 g; Dietary Fibre 8 g; Cholesterol 79.5 mg; 2425 kJ (580 Cal)

1

2

3

CHINESE ROAST DUCK WITH FRESH PAPPARDELLE

Preparation time: 15 minutes
Cooking time: 10 minutes
Serves 4–6

250 g (9 oz) baby bok choy (pak choi), washed and leaves separated
600 g (1 lb 5 oz) fresh pappardelle
1 Chinese roast duck, skin removed (see Note)
80 ml (1/3 cup) peanut oil
3 garlic cloves, crushed
3 teaspoons finely chopped fresh ginger
35 g (3/4 cup) chopped fresh coriander (cilantro) leaves
2 tablespoons hoisin sauce
2 tablespoons oyster sauce

1 Bring a large saucepan of water to the boil and blanch the bok choy for 1–2 minutes, or until tender, but still crisp. Remove with a slotted spoon and keep warm. In the same pan of boiling water, cook the pasta until *al dente*. Drain well and keep warm.
2 Remove the duck meat from the bones and finely shred. Heat the peanut oil in a small saucepan over high heat and bring it up to smoking point. Remove from the heat and allow to cool for 1 minute, then swirl in the garlic and ginger to infuse the oil. Be careful not to allow the garlic to burn or it will turn bitter.
3 Pour the hot oil over the pasta and add the bok choy, duck, coriander, hoisin and oyster sauces. Toss well, season and serve immediately.

NUTRITION PER SERVE (6)
Fat 19.5 g; Protein 29 g; Carbohydrate 75.5 g; Dietary Fibre 4.5 g; Cholesterol 104.5 mg; 2490 kJ (595 Cal)

COOK'S FILE
Note: Chinese roast duck can be bought from Asian barbecue food shops or restaurants.

1

2

3

CREAMY VEAL WITH MUSHROOMS

Preparation time: 15 minutes
Cooking time: 30 minutes
Serves 4

100 g (3½ oz) butter
500 g (1 lb 2 oz) veal schnitzel, cut into 3 cm (1¼ inch) pieces
300 g (10½ oz) Swiss brown mushrooms, sliced
3 garlic cloves, crushed
185 ml (¾ cup) dry white wine
125 ml (½ cup) chicken stock
200 ml (7 fl oz) thick (double/heavy) cream
1–2 tablespoons lemon juice
400 g (14 oz) pappardelle

1 Melt half the butter in a large frying pan over medium heat. Add the veal in batches and cook for 2–3 minutes, or until golden brown. Remove the veal from the pan and keep warm.

2 Add the remaining butter to the same pan and heat until foaming. Add the mushrooms and garlic and cook, stirring, over low heat for 5 minutes. Pour in the wine and stock, scraping the bottom of the pan with a wooden spoon, and simmer, covered, for 10 minutes. Remove the lid, add the cream and simmer for 5 minutes, or until the sauce thickens. Stir in the lemon juice, veal and any juices until warmed through. Season to taste. Meanwhile, cook the pasta in a large saucepan of boiling water until *al dente*. Toss the sauce through the pasta and serve immediately.

NUTRITION PER SERVE
Fat 40.5 g; Protein 45 g; Carbohydrate 74 g; Dietary Fibre 5 g; Cholesterol 235.5 mg; 3660 kJ (875 Cal)

1

2

PAPPARDELLE WITH FRESH SALMON AND GREMOLATA

Preparation time: 15 minutes
Cooking time: 15 minutes
Serves 4

30 g (½ cup) chopped fresh flat-leaf
  (Italian) parsley
3 teaspoons grated lemon zest
2 garlic cloves, finely chopped
400 g (14 oz) pappardelle
60 ml (¼ cup) extra virgin olive oil
500 g (1 lb 2 oz) fresh salmon fillet
2 teaspoons olive oil, extra

1 To make the gremolata, put the parsley, lemon zest and garlic in a bowl and mix together well. Cook the pasta in a large saucepan of boiling water until *al dente*. Drain, return to the pan, then add the olive oil and toss gently. Add the gremolata to the bowl with the pasta and toss again.

2 Remove the skin and any bones from the salmon. Heat the extra olive oil in a frying pan and cook the salmon over medium heat for 3–4 minutes, turning once during cooking. Take care not to overcook the fish. Flake the salmon into large pieces and toss through the pasta. Season to taste with salt and ground black pepper, divide among four warm serving plates and serve.

NUTRITION PER SERVE
Fat 24.5 g; Protein 37.5 g; Carbohydrate 70.5 g; Dietary Fibre 3.5 g; Cholesterol 83 mg; 2755 kJ (660 Cal)

1

2

STRACCI WITH ARTICHOKES AND CHARGRILLED CHICKEN

Preparation time: 10 minutes
Cooking time: 20 minutes
Serves 6

1 tablespoon olive oil
3 chicken breast fillets
500 g (1 lb 2 oz) stracci
8 slices prosciutto
280 g (10 oz) jar artichokes in oil, drained and quartered, and oil reserved
150 g (5½ oz) semi-dried (sun-blushed) tomatoes, thinly sliced
80 g (2¾ oz) baby rocket (arugula) leaves
2–3 tablespoons balsamic vinegar

1 Lightly brush a chargrill or frying pan with the oil and heat over high heat. Cook the chicken for 6–8 minutes each side, or until cooked through. Cut into thin slices on the diagonal. Set aside.

2 Cook the pasta in a large saucepan of boiling water until *al dente*. Meanwhile, place the prosciutto on a lined grill tray and cook under a hot grill for 2 minutes each side, or until crisp. Cool slightly and break into pieces. Drain the pasta, then combine with the chicken, prosciutto, artichokes, tomato and rocket in a bowl and toss. Whisk together 60 ml (¼ cup) of the reserved artichoke oil and the balsamic vinegar and toss through the pasta mixture. Season to taste with salt and ground black pepper, then serve.

NUTRITION PER SERVE
Fat 9 g; Protein 30 g; Carbohydrate 51 g; Dietary Fibre 4 g; Cholesterol 103 mg; 1705 kJ (410 Cal)

SEAFOOD LASAGNE

Preparation time: 15 minutes
Cooking time: 15 minutes
Serves 4

1 tablespoon olive oil
2 garlic cloves, crushed
1/4 teaspoon saffron threads
600 g (1 lb 5 oz) bottled tomato
    pasta sauce
750 g (1 lb 10 oz) mixed raw seafood,
    cut into 3 cm (1 1/4 inch) pieces
    (use scallops and peeled
    prawns/shrimp or prepared
    marinara mix)
120 g (4 oz) English spinach
    leaves

200 g (7 oz) fresh lasagne sheets (4),
    cut into twelve 10 x 16 cm
    (4 x 6 1/2 inch) rectangles
165 g (3/4 cup) mascarpone
75 g (3/4 cup) grated Parmesan cheese

1 Heat the oil in a large saucepan, add the garlic, saffron and pasta sauce, reduce the heat and simmer for 8 minutes, or until it thickens slightly. Add the seafood and cook for 2 minutes, or until cooked, then season. Remove from the heat.

2 Blanch the spinach in a large saucepan of boiling water for 30 seconds. Remove with tongs, transfer to a colander and drain well. Cook the pasta in the same saucepan of boiling water for 1–2 minutes, or until *al dente*. Remove and arrange the sheets individually on a tray to prevent them sticking.

3 To assemble, lay a pasta rectangle on four ovenproof serving plates. Use half the mascarpone to spread over the pasta sheets. Top with half the spinach leaves and half the seafood sauce. Sprinkle with one third of the Parmesan. Repeat to give two layers, finishing with a third pasta sheet. Sprinkle with the remaining cheese. Place under a medium grill (broiler) for 2 minutes, or until the cheese is slightly melted. Serve immediately.

NUTRITION PER SERVE
Fat 28.5 g; Protein 52.5 g; Carbohydrate 47 g; Dietary Fibre 5 g; Cholesterol 364 mg; 2750 kJ (655 Cal)

1

2

3

BEETROOT RAVIOLI WITH A SAGE BURNT BUTTER

Preparation time: 15 minutes
Cooking time: 10 minutes
Serves 4

340 g (11½ oz) jar baby beetroots in sweet vinegar
40 g (1½ oz) grated Parmesan cheese
250 g (9 oz) fresh ricotta cheese
750 g (1 lb 10 oz) fresh lasagne sheets (4 sheets)
fine cornmeal, for sprinkling
200 g (7 oz) butter, chopped
5 g (¼ cup) fresh sage, torn
2 garlic cloves, crushed

1 Drain the beetroot, then grate it into a bowl. Add the Parmesan and ricotta and mix well. Lay a sheet of pasta on a flat surface and place evenly spaced tablespoons of the ricotta mixture on the pasta to give 12 mounds—four across and three down. Flatten the mounds of filling slightly. Lightly brush the edges of the pasta sheet and around each pile of ricotta mix with water.

2 Place a second sheet of pasta over the top and gently press around each mound to seal and enclose the filling. Using a pasta wheel or sharp knife, cut the pasta into 12 ravioli. Lay them out separately on a lined tray that has been sprinkled with the cornmeal. Repeat with the remaining filling and lasagne sheets to make 24 ravioli. Gently remove any excess air bubbles after cutting so that they are completely sealed.

3 Cook the pasta in a large saucepan of boiling water until *al dente*. Drain, divide among four serving plates and keep warm. Melt the butter in a saucepan and cook for 3–4 minutes, or until golden brown. Remove from the heat, stir in the sage and garlic and spoon over the ravioli. Sprinkle with shaved Parmesan, if desired, and season with pepper.

NUTRITION PER SERVE
Fat 52 g; Protein 15.5 g; Carbohydrate 32.5 g; Dietary Fibre 3 g; Cholesterol 167.5 mg; 2720 kJ (650 Cal)

1

2

3

WARM PASTA AND SMOKED SALMON STACK

Preparation time: 15 minutes
Cooking time: 15 minutes
Serves 4

1.5 kg (3 lb 5 oz) vine-ripened
    tomatoes
2 garlic cloves, crushed
1 teaspoon sugar
80 ml (⅓ cup) good-quality olive oil
3 tablespoons chopped fresh
    flat-leaf (Italian) parsley
6 fresh lasagne sheets
400 g (14 oz) smoked salmon
100 g (3½ oz) baby rocket (arugula)
    leaves
extra virgin olive oil, for drizzling

1 Score a cross in the base of each tomato and place them in a bowl of boiling water for 1 minute. Plunge into cold water and peel the skin away from the cross. Remove the core, then transfer to a food processor or blender and, using the pulse button, process until roughly chopped. Transfer to a saucepan with the garlic and sugar, bring to the boil, then reduce the heat and simmer for 5 minutes, or until reduced slightly. Remove from the heat and gradually whisk in the oil. Stir in the parsley and season. Keep warm.

2 Cut the lasagne sheets in half widthways to give 12 pieces, each about 12 cm (5 inch) square. Cook the pasta in a large saucepan of boiling water in two batches until *al dente*. Remove from the water and lay out flat separately to prevent sticking. Place a pasta sheet on four plates. Set aside 80 ml (⅓ cup) of the tomato mix. Spoon half the remaining tomato mixture over the pasta sheets, then half the smoked salmon and rocket leaves. Repeat to give two layers. Finish with a third sheet of pasta. Top each pasta stack with a tablespoon of the tomato sauce, drizzle with a little extra virgin olive oil and serve immediately.

NUTRITION PER SERVE
Fat 24.5 g; Protein 32 g; Carbohydrate 36.5 g; Dietary Fibre 6.5 g; Cholesterol 48 mg; 2065 kJ (495 Cal)

TUNA AND CHERMOULA ON PAPPARDELLE

Preparation time: 15 minutes +
  20 minutes marinating
Cooking time: 30 minutes
Serves 4

500 g (1 lb 2 oz) sweet potato, cut
  into 2 cm (³/4 inch) cubes
100 ml (3¹/2 fl oz) olive oil
60 g (2 cups) fresh coriander (cilantro)
  leaves, finely chopped
40 g (2 cups) fresh flat-leaf (Italian)
  parsley, chopped
3 garlic cloves, crushed
3 teaspoons ground cumin
60 ml (¹/4 cup) lemon juice
4 x 180 g (6 oz) tuna steaks
400 g (14 oz) pappardelle

1 Preheat the oven to 200°C (400°F/Gas 6). Toss the sweet potato in 2 tablespoons of the oil, place on a baking tray and roast for 25–30 minutes, or until tender.
2 To make the chermoula, place the coriander, parsley, garlic, cumin and ³/4 teaspoon cracked black pepper in a small food processor and process until a rough paste forms. Transfer to a bowl and stir in the lemon juice and 1 tablespoon of the oil. Place the tuna in a non-metallic bowl, cover with 2 tablespoons of the chermoula and toss until it is evenly coated. Marinate in the refrigerator for 20 minutes. Meanwhile, cook the pasta in a large saucepan of boiling water until *al dente*. Drain, return to the pan and mix in the remaining chermoula and oil. Keep warm.
3 Heat a lightly oiled chargrill pan over high heat. Cook the tuna for 2 minutes each side, or until done to your liking. Cut into 2 cm (³/4 inch) cubes, toss through the pasta with the sweet potato and serve.

NUTRITION PER SERVE
Fat 34 g; Protein 62 g; Carbohydrate 89.5 g; Dietary Fibre 7 g; Cholesterol 83 mg; 3830 kJ (915 Cal)

1

2

3

QUICK MUSHROOM AND RICOTTA CANNELLONI

Preparation time: 15 minutes
Cooking time: 30 minutes
Serves 4

500 g (1 lb 2 oz) button mushrooms
200 g (7 oz) fresh lasagne sheets
2 tablespoons olive oil
3 garlic cloves, crushed
2 tablespoons lemon juice
400 g (14 oz) fresh ricotta cheese
3 tablespoons chopped fresh
    basil
425 g (15 oz) bottled tomato pasta
    sauce
150 g (1 cup) grated mozzarella
    cheese

1 Preheat the oven to 180°C (350°F/Gas 4). Place the mushrooms in a food processor and pulse until finely chopped. Cut the lasagne sheets into twelve 13 x 16 cm (5 x 6½ inch) rectangles.

2 Heat the oil in a large frying pan over medium heat. Add the garlic and mushrooms and cook, stirring, for 3 minutes. Add the lemon juice and cook for 2 minutes, or until softened. Transfer to a sieve over a bowl to collect the juices, pressing with a spoon to remove as much moisture as possible. Reserve.

3 Combine the mushrooms, ricotta and basil. Season well. Place heaped tablespoons of the mixture along one long edge of the lasagne sheet. Roll up, then place in a greased 2 litre (8 cup) 16 x 30 cm (6½ x 12 inch) ovenproof ceramic dish. Repeat with the remaining mixture and sheets, placing them in a single layer. Pour on the reserved mushroom cooking liquid, then pour on the pasta sauce. Sprinkle with cheese and bake for 25 minutes, or until golden and bubbling. Serve with salad.

NUTRITION PER SERVE
Fat 29.5 g; Protein 32.5 g; Carbohydrate 37.5 g; Dietary Fibre 6 g; Cholesterol 90 mg; 2290 kJ (545 Cal)

1

2

3

INDEX

INTERNATIONAL GLOSSARY OF INGREDIENTS

chilli	chili pepper, chile	fresh coriander	fresh cilantro
eggplant	aubergine	tomato purée (Aus.)	sieved crushed tomatoes/ passata (UK)
tomato paste (Aus.)	tomato purée, double concentrate (UK)	zucchini	courgette

This edition published in 2008 by Bay Books, an imprint of Murdoch Books Pty Limited. Pier 8/9, 23 Hickson Road, Millers Point, NSW, 2000, Australia.

Managing Editor: Rachel Carter **Editors:** Zoë Harpham **Creative Director:** Marylouise Brammer **Designer:** Michelle Cutler **Food Director:** Jane Lawson **Food Editor:** Rebecca Clancy **Recipe Development:** Alison Adams, Ruth Armstrong, Rebecca Clancy, Ross Dobson, Michelle Earl, Jo Glynn, Fiona Hammond, Kay Holder, Kathy Knudsen, Jane Lawson, Michelle Lawton, Valli Little, Barbara Lowery, Kate Murdoch, Christine Osmond, Sally Parker, Wendy Quisumbing, Melita Smilovic, Angla Tregonning **Home Economists:** Justine Johnson, Valli Little, Evelyn Morris, Kate Murdoch, Kim Passenger, Angela Tregonning **Photographers:** Jo Filshie, Reg Morrison (steps) **Food Stylist:** Georgina Dolling **Food Preparation:** Justine Poole, Christine Sheppard (cover) **Nutritionist:** Dr Susanna Holt **Index:** Puddingburn Publishing Serivces **UK Consultant:** Maggi Altham
Chief Executive: Juliet Rogers. **Publisher:** Kay Scarlett.

The nutritional information provided for each recipe does not include garnishes or accompaniments, such as rice, unless they are included in specific quantities in the ingredients. The values are approximations and can be affected by biological and seasonal variations in food, the unknown composition of some manufactured foods and uncertainty in the dietary database. Nutrient data given are derived primarily from the NUTTAB95 database produced by the Australian New Zealand Food Authority.

ISBN 978 0 681 24542 6
Printed by Sing Cheong Printing Co. Ltd. PRINTED IN CHINA.